# Making Use of History in New South African Fiction

*Sten Pultz Moslund*

# Making Use of History in New South African Fiction

An Analysis of the Purposes of Historical Perspectives in Three Post-Apartheid Novels

Museum Tusculanum Press
University of Copenhagen
2003

S. Pultz Moslund, *Making Use of History in New South African Fiction*
© 2003 Museum Tusculanum Press & the author
Consultants: Michael Jackson & Sven Engelbrecht
Cover design by Veronique van der Neut
Composition by Ole Klitgaard
ISBN 87 7289 784 8
Printed in Denmark

Cover illustration:
Willie Bester: "The truth and reconciliation"
Mixed media collage, 1999 (80 × 123 cm)
Copyright: Studio d'Arte Raffaelli, Trento (Italy)

Published with support from
G.E.C. Gads Fond
Nordea Danmark Fonden

Museum Tusculanum Press
Njalsgade 92
DK-2300 Copenhagen S
www.mtp.dk

# Table of Contents

Acknowledgements ................................................... 7

Introduction ................................................................ 9

Mongane Wally Serote: *Gods of Our Time* ............................ 36

Resistant Form in *Gods of Our Time* ..................................... 55

Mike Nicol: *The Ibis Tapestry* ................................................ 62

Resistant Form in *The Ibis Tapestry* ........................................ 83

Zakes Mda: *Ways of Dying* ..................................................... 90

Resistant Form in *Ways of Dying* ........................................... 114

Conclusion ............................................................................. 118

Notes ....................................................................................... 125

Bibliography .......................................................................... 131

*To my father*

# Acknowledgements

I am greatly indebted to Malcolm Hacksley and the National English Literary Museum in South Africa for assisting me in all respects during the process of writing the manuscript for this book. Furthermore, I am much obliged to Sven Engelbrecht for his excellent supervision of the project and generous help in the search of funding. In respect of the latter, I also owe a special thanks to Holger Bernt Hansen and the Centre of Africa Studies at the University of Copenhagen. I am grateful for the financial support of the book provided by G.E.C. Gads Fond and Nordea Danmark Fonden. I wish to thank Marianne Alenius at the Museum of Tusculanum Press for encouraging me and demonstrating such a strong belief in the subjects of this book. Finally, I am forever grateful for the patience and invaluable support of Marie, my companion in life.

# Introduction

*The Past is knocking constantly on the doors of our perceptions, refusing to be forgotten, because it is deeply embedded in the present. To neglect it at this most crucial of moments in our history is to postpone the future*
                    –Njabulo Ndebele (1994: 158).

Although history as a discourse has entered our minds persuasively as a factual and truthful conveyer of the plain reality of the past, history can never escape being a discourse with substantial interests in the present. Studies of history and historicism have made it increasingly clear that history as social memory is customarily changed and transformed in order to preserve or generate a certain social identity that may endorse the realisation of imminent social, political or economic visions. Although such uses pretend to be speaking of the reality of the past, this is far from the case. The past is rarely, if ever, allowed to stand on its own by and for itself, but is systematically tailored by the present to suit its purposes.

"Historians are second only to atomic scientists as threats to humanity". With reference to the genocide in Rwanda this claim was staked by René Lemarchand at a seminar in Copenhagen (Lemarchand, 1999). The point of the provocative statement is that certain uses of history have always been, and continue to be, the principal vehicles of pitting communities against one another in unimaginable sprees of destruction and violence. The reason why history is used for such purposes pertains to the cardinal role of historical narratives – whether these appear in official accounts, academic historiography or, as is the focus of this book, in historical literature – which is that of constructing or confirming collective identities. One of the most important objects of history's political utilisation is to establish what Benedict Anderson calls "imagined communities". The past is used, manipulated and forged to create within a group of people, be it a nation or a subnational ethnic fraction, a strong sense of standing together as a collective, coherent, homogenous group that by some natural virtue thinks and acts in unison. According to Anderson, nationalism, or, for that matter, any other formation of group identity, invariably uses a distant, immemorial, mythic past as a point of reference that confirms its unique existence, its primordial status, as put by Anderson, its "self-evident plausibility" (Anderson, 1991: 12).

As much as such basic political utilisation of historical narratives may exist for peaceful purposes in fairly free and well-functioning societies, an arbitrary glance at the course of the world reveals how commonly historical narratives are exploited in legitimising the oppressive, aggressive or intolerant politics of totalitarian systems and ideas. In the context of the latter, history's own history is one of being employed by totalitarian institutions either to suppress or to produce differences within a society. Authoritarian regimes typically assume absolute control of defining the boundaries of power and the values of the national character or group identity. They do so by imposing monological versions of the past on society that authorise the contemporary order as the inevitable and predetermined conclusion of historical cause and effect.

To start out with an example from Morocco, the past is exploited in the official discourse to harmonise national identity and national tenets in convergence with the rule of the monarchy. The present king, Mohammed VI, and his predecessor Hassan II, have consciously manipulated an inseparable link between the monarchy and the independence struggle against the French colonial regime in the 1950s in order to legitimise the continued rule of the Alawi dynasty and to discourage popular support of voices calling for human rights and a *de facto* democracy. Likewise, the Alawi dynasti grants itself primordial legitimacy by claiming to be the direct descendants of the Prophet Muhammad (Boserup, 2001: 1-5). Public buildings in Morocco repeatedly remind the Moroccans of the hallowed position of the present rule by repeating on every facade the old slogan of the struggle *Allah, al-watan, al-malik* (God, the nation, the king) (4-5). In this way, the Alawi dynasty has exploited its institutional power to shroud itself in a persuasive discourse that claims the roots of Moroccan identity to itself – the freedom struggle, the independent state and religion. When the fatalism of the official discourse has consolidated itself sufficiently in the public mindset, it becomes extremely difficult to think in terms of alternative realities. In the minds of many Moroccans, it becomes an act of self-effacement to oppose the system as it would be "un-Moroccan" to separate the king from the government and un-Islamic to separate the king from the Prophet. Any attempt to think differently will have to persuade people of the existence of an entirely different reality produced by an entirely different past.

A similar strategy of conforming national identity is discernible in a number of the official narratives of Latin American dictatorships. In Brazil, military hard-liners staged a coup within a coup, as a culmination of the country's historical succession of autocratic regimes and unstable governments, and gained de facto dictatorial powers between 1969 and 1974. History's role in the rhetoric of the new regime was to establish a sense of national unity and pride that would justify the state's oppressive practices as a necessary evil for the sake of the common good. A "national myth" was generated of a historical continuity that had eventually produced a particular Brazilian character based on "syncreticism, the love of harmony and the innate cordiality and benevolence of the Brazilian people", while the reality of conflict and of Brazil's complex cultural and religious make-up was repressed in the collective narrative (Valente, 1993: 43, 44, 53).

The other way round, history may also be chartered and censored from above to bolster a problematic or unpopular rule by creating differences within the masses, the identification of a collective enemy or the invention of a scapegoat being essential measures for buttressing authoritarian politics and strengthening political loyalty. In the process, human reality and existence becomes based entirely on the belief in categorical demarcations between the inclusive world of truth, necessity, morality and an excluded world of the Other as unwanted, false, extraneous and foreign. Consecrating differences with historical importance has proved itself extremely effective in mobilising people to act against those who are "different" or "threatening" towards the narrative that keeps the collective together.

In Rwanda 1994, history played a crucial part in mobilising Hutus to decimate their Tutsi countrymen. What Liisa Malkki terms *mythico-histories* were ingeniously fabricated out of the country's past and mass communicated by the Hutu leadership to forge absolute and antagonistic ethnic borders with the result that a comparatively harmonious, culturally complex society was mangled by mass murder (Lemarchand, 1999 and Uvin, 1997). According to Malkki, a mythico-history is a particular, collectivised, narrative of the past that comprises more than a mere description or evaluation of the past. It is a narrative that subversively recasts and reinterprets the past in *fundamentally moral terms*, categorising the past into a elementary frame of loaded opposition between agents of good and agents of evil[1] (Malkki, 1995: 54). The complexity of the history of Rwandese ethnicities was thus simplified and demonised to suit a grand moral dictum of Tutsi cruelty and Hutu victimisation. The Tutsi were said to have intruded Hutu territory in the distant past and subsequently to have prompted a historical continuation of inhuman Tutsi domination over a subjugated and essentially violated Hutu serfdom (54).

The dialectic between histories of compulsory unity and essentialised differences invariably comes to the fore when regimes shift, when for example the homogenising control of centralised power collapses and repressed identities are extricated. After the 1972 massacre of Hutus in Burundi, the Tutsi sought to erase the past from the collective consciousness by denying any notion of animosity within the populace and forbidding any reference to ethnic identities, starting with the history lessons in primary schools (Lemarchand, 1996: 5-7). When Burundi's first Hutu president, Melchior Ndadaye, was assassinated in 1993 by an all-Tutsi army, the repressed memory of 1972 resurfaced and became the vehicle of another eruption of violence.

Correspondingly, in many ex-Communist countries, the power vacuum left by the implosion of the Soviet Union has produced a resurgence of previously subordinated ethnic identities. To mention a lesser known case than the balkanisation of former Yugoslavia, the Central Asian countries of Kazakhstan, Kyrgyzstan, Tadzikhistan, Turkmenistan and Uzbekistan experience the revival of narratives that trace the evolution of modern national groups, like Tadzhiks, Armenians, Azerbaizhanis, Turkmen, Uzbeks, Kazakhs, Kyrgyz, from pre-history to their present form in order to legitimise group-based contentions for power. The question is whether these new mythico histories will mobilise separatist feelings and balkanise the region as in ex-Yugoslavia or new, representative political systems will be able to establish themselves as a positively unifying power (Akiner, 1997).

Turning to the particular area of study in this book, history has been pivotal in the construction and maintenance of apartheid. As such, the uses of the past have had the dual function of both strengthening narratives of collectivity while simultaneously splitting the population into fixed categories.

The apartheid state was founded on the construction of Afrikaner nationalism. The historical experience of the first Dutch settlers, the Great Trek, the battles with African tribes, Afrikaner suffering and heroism in the Anglo-Boer war were mythologised into a grand narrative of common experience that consolidated a collective Afrikaner identity as historically rooted, homogenous and pure and the demarcations between the races as authentic and primordial (Brink, 1998: 36). A collective amnesia was produced on issues of class differences and other diversities within the Afrikaner population as well as on the great dependency, collaboration, social and sexual interaction that also characterised the relations between Afrikaners, Coloureds and Africans. The differentiation Afrikaner nationalism created within the white population by setting itself off on the historical conflicts with the English was counterbalanced by racist ideology and an emphasis on South Africa's history of segregation. Common interest was strengthened and cultivated by centralising a discourse of natural competition between white people and other races, shrinking nationalist distinctions between the Afrikaners and the English from a political to a cultural level.

In the 1960s, the grand scheme of turning South Africa into a white state by resettling the entire African population in independent states constructed for the purpose, the so-called "Bantustans" or "homelands", gained support by another myth of historical rooting. The plan of converting the 13 percent of South Africa's entire land area allotted to Africans in the 1913 and 1936 Land Acts into ten tribal states was vindicated as an honourable attempt to restore the territories to the respective black "nations" that, allegedly, had occupied these territories in pre-colonial history (Cornevin, 1980: 121). Together with the idealisation of racial and ethnic purity and their need for "separate development", the apartheid state felt it had provided sufficient historical and rational justification to "repatriate" and retribalise the African population thus uprooting and separating an estimated 3.5 million people by forced removals between 1960 and 1983 (Worden, 1996: 111).

Moreover, to lessen domestic resistance and international criticism, white supremacy justified itself through a manipulated myth of origin, turned into an official apartheid doctrine, which stated that the white man arrived in South Africa to uninhabited land, thus being naturally entitled to the place. The myth deprived Africans of their right to land and delineated them as immigrants settling on white territory[2] (Cornevin, 1980: 78). A related myth stated that the expansion of the Afrikaners into the interior of South Africa was equally legitimate. The *Voortrekkers* arrived in an uninhabited land that had been depopulated by Zulu aggression during the tribal wars of the *Difaqane* (101).

Apparently, on the reverse side of these dictating histories, aberrant or autonomous histories, representing alternative realities, are subdued or effaced. In apartheid South Africa, as in all dictatorial regimes, the social and political reality brought about by the official myths was sustained with ruthless repression of any form of challenging ideas. Censorship and the distortion of news by the regime led to a tremendous amount of blank spots and misrepresentations in South African history. Apartheid schoolbooks, for example, said nothing about slavery and the media said nothing about the conditions in the homelands and in the township nor of the daily measures of coercion, torture and assassinations (Ward and Worden, 1998: 202-3).

The experience of being crushed by authoritarian grand narratives, is, as anthropologist Michael Jackson says in his study of the nature and politics of storytelling, an experience of being *overwhelmed* by external forces, whether the forces be external to the individual or to a marginalised group of people. When motivated by equitable power relations, we alternate between different roles in our daily human interactions of being active controllers of events and being acted upon. Conversely, as soon as one narrative assumes absolute control, the usually oscillating power relations are frozen into a fixed constellation of authority and subordination. When subordinated by an authoritarian narrative and its material consequences, one is objectified by public discourse from being a "who" to being entirely a "what" – from, says Jackson, "a subject who actively participates in the making or unmaking of his or her world" to "a subject who suffers and is subjected to actions by others", by "forces of circumstance, that lie largely outside his or her control" (Jackson, 2002: 2).

Being overpowered and objectified by external circumstances is at odds with human nature. Everybody needs to experience that they have some kind of influence on their own situation, to feel some sense of self-determination. "In spite of…the contingencies of history, the tyranny of circumstance, the finality of death, and the accidents of fate", Jackson maintains, "every human being needs some modicum of choice, craves some degree of understanding, demands some say, and expects some sense of control over the course of his or her own life". In other words, everybody needs at least "a *sense* of agency", an opportunity to "*imagine* that one's life belongs to a matrix greater than oneself, and that within this sphere of greater Being one's own actions and words matter and make a difference" (Jackson, 2002: 4).

This is where the importance of counter-histories becomes apparent; the histories that emerge when the objectified, the Othered, the oppressed assume the power of definition and assert realities, of past and present, that refute or challenge the master narrative. Whether counter histories take the form of historical revisionism, the recuperation of the silenced past, witness testimonies, biographical accounts or other attempts to counter the dictates of official scripts with alternative pasts, counter-histories involve a conscious attempt to regain the command of one's own reality. Accordingly, the distribution of other myths of origin, a victim's account, a newspaper article on state violation or the expression of a marginalised perspective may comprise a complex "vital human strategy for sustaining a sense of agency in the face of disempowering circumstances" (Jackson, 2002: 4). Counter-histories may rework and restructure the past psychologically, socially and metaphorically to change our experience and perception of truth and the limits of reality. Or counter-histories simply allow events, truths and realities to exist by making them known and by calling them forth from the darkness and silence of repression and censorship. By telling our own hi-/ stories, we take centre stage, says Michael Jackson. We enable ourselves to "rework[ ] and remodel[ ] subject-object relations in ways that subtly alter the balance between actor and acted upon, thus allowing us to feel that we actively participate in a world that for a moment seemed to discount, demean, and disempower us" (4-6). In short, the act of joining the contention of naming the past and the present carries the promise and the opportunity of envisioning and making other future realities possible in which one can exercise one's right to influence.

In Morocco, the public narrative legitimising the monarchy as the self-evident and naturally recognised authority of the Moroccan people is countered by witness testimonies of political repression. Evelyn Serfaty, Ali Bourequat, Driss Benzekri, Ahmed Marzouki and other former political prisoners of Hasan II's authoritarian rule document how they were sentenced and tortured for their alternative visions of government, thus inflicting breaches in the official myth by making known what the official myth attempted to silence (Boserup, 2001: 13). The witness accounts are directly and indirectly used to put pressure on the current power structure and to mobilise support for political change in the country by calling attention to the absence of human rights and democracy. Hence, the uses of these accounts of repressed pasts span from outspoken rejections of the forged links between the monarchy and the struggle for an independent Moroccan nation, by associating the Alawi dynasty with a continuation of European imperialism, to summoning a history of violation as a moral point of departure that may reinterpret and reform the present and the future (Boserup, 2001).

In Brazil, victims of political repression have also voiced versions of reality that undermine the collective definitions of identity as proposed by the junta of 1969. As in Morocco, these versions are typically mediated through memorialist accounts in the autobiographical genre that cast light on an organisation of institutionalised terror directed against political dissidents. In addition, because Brazilian counter-histories written during the repression had to circumvent the constraints of ubiquitous censorship, many subversive versions of state repression resorted to allegory and symbolism. A writer like João Ubaldo Ribeiro sought to mimic state repression by having fictional gunmen hunt down the political enemies of obscure authorities and he employed satire to deflate the pompous official rhetoric of a mythologised Brazilian national character (Valente, 1993: 43-4).

The capacity of other histories of injuring hegemonic narratives is also exploited by organised resistance movements in mobilising people against the oppressor. In South Africa, counter-histories played an important role in the mobilisation of the resistance against white minority rule. Since the 1950s, and in particular during the rise of Black Consciousness in the 1970s, the resistance movement made an effort in countering the state myths of apartheid by exposing the process of white invasion and conquest followed by dispossession, enslavement, segregation and disenfranchisement of non-white South Africans (Cornevin, 1980: 130). The purpose was to discredit the apartheid regime's justification of itself internationally, but even more so to make the oppressed realise the extent of their oppression in order for them to engage in changing the existing power structure.

In the anti-apartheid line of the 1980s, the project of writing alternative histories was consciously located as a vehicle of empowerment within the popular resistance narratives and the cultural politics of nationalism. The counter-histories produced by the nation-wide coalition of anti-apartheid organisations, the United Democratic Front (UDF), were guided by key objectives such as "history from below", "people's history", "people's power" and "people's education". Methodologically, these alternative histories sought to counter silence and censorship by re-constructing collective memories with multiple individual remembrances. In Johannesburg a history of the formations of classes and class consciousness was reconstructed, in Natal biographies of ordinary people mapped out the development of organised resistance, and in Capetown, a nostalgia of common people's experiences assembled a picture of a community splintered by state intervention and forced removals. Altogether, these histories accumulated a grand narrative of experience which in form and content was marked by political protest and transformatory intent (Minkley and Rassool, 1998: 92-4).

Another side to the South African counter histories was to resist the state ideology of ethnic purity. In order to prevent any fragmentation of the resistance movement, the significance of symbols of cultural tradition and ethnic differences were downplayed by the rhetoric of the resistance movement, even to the extent that ethnicity was condemned entirely as an identity marker to prevent any fragmentation of the collective struggle. The only exception to this was the Zulu movement of Inkatha, spearheaded by Mangusuto Buthelezi who gained covert state support, political status and coherency within the movement by playing the ethnic card of essentialising Zulu commitment in a world of group rivalry.

Ranajit Guha has, among other critics of historiography, called attention to the fact that the subaltern and the representation of the subaltern in historiography are disposed to be at odds with each other. Historiography as a supposedly scientific discipline[3] has evolved from and been developed within the official domain of the power holders and the social elite and as such it has been naturally inclined to operate at a political and sociological distance from the subject masses. In colonial India, history served as a vehicle of the imperial authorities and the rebellions against colonial oppression were represented in history, accordingly, with a Eurocentric bias. For instance, as Guha points out in his study of blank spots in Indian historiography, the narrative of insurgency in colonial India, as it has been handed down to the present in the written records of Indian History, does not accredit any political motivation or rationality to the subaltern agents nor does it offer the voices and perspectives of the actual rebels. Not surprisingly, colonial historians never even considered the possibility of a political consciousness as the originator and motivator of peasant rebellions. Guha's studies show how they treated rebellions almost by default as a "matter to be explained in terms of natural history". In the terminology of these historians uprisings broke out spontaneously, haphazardly, contagiously, chaotically like natural disasters and epidemics (Guha, 1983: 2). Likewise, through the self-justifying looking glass of the Eurocentric historian, rebellions were expressions of a failure of the lesser races to realise the benevolence of the civilising enterprise. In the process, the signifiers of popular resistance in colonial historiography were inverted from a worthy disposition of overthrowing injustice to a dark, motiveless outburst of violent irrationality and savagery jeopardising a humane order of things (19). Even critical historians very rarely looked for explanations in factors such as economic and political deprivation, describing rebellion, rather, as instinctive and mindless responses to physical suffering (3).

The ensuing historical schools of Indian nationalism and Marxist historicism have countered the misrepresentation of the Other in colonial historiography, but being written by the social elites, these histories also fail to record the peasant revolts without consideration for their own ideological precepts. Guha shows how the bourgeois source of Indian nationalist historiography reiterates the disregard in colonial historiography of a political consciousness among the subaltern masses; it, too, "excludes the rebel as the conscious subject of his own history" (32-3). Rather, they read their own ideals into the peasant movements by emphasising the role of the elitist leaders as the great initiators who transferred political awareness to the otherwise unconscious masses (38). Although Marxist historians have not failed to consider the political awareness among peasant rebels, they still fall short in representing the subaltern. Owing to the incompatibility of political consciousness and religion in Marxist thinking, Guha argues, the Marxist school fails to recognise religion as a crucial factor in mass mobilisation of Indian peasant revolts and as an important element in rebel consciousness (38).

Obviously, the subaltern have had no direct access to representing themselves in established discourses of authority and as such they have had very little opportunity to participate in the construction of the official narrative. However, the exclusion of Other narratives from participation in narrating official histories has not prevented them from emerging. Rather, they find their way forward in other genres than the strictly historiographical. Among these genres is fiction.

In Morocco the mentioned auto-/biographical accounts of state violation are accompanied by several histories mediated through literary genres. Aziz Wadîa, for example, uses poetry to expresses the concern of unachieved freedom by rejecting the connection between the throne and the struggle for independence and exposing, instead, the similarities between the post-independent rule and that of the French colonisers. Through satire and sarcasm, Wadîa also employs his poetry to reverse the power relation between tortured and torturer by providing the former with the superiority of definition in ridiculing the parochialism and the baseness of the latter. Abelaziz Mouride's *On affame bien les rats!* is a documentary "cartoon" that images and collectivises the author's recollections of torture during ten years of imprisonment (Boserup, 2001: 16-17). Not only do these drawings image and visualise an institution that has been unknown to the public because of its repression by the official narratives – not a single photo of the prison exists – they also make the alternative version of the past accessible to a much larger part of Moroccans than written works, given the country's high rates of illiteracy.

João Ubaldo Ribeiro's use of literature in circumventing censorship has already been mentioned as an example of counter-history in Brazilian fiction. Successively, after the institutionalisation of democracy, fiction in Brazil has been preoccupied with the search for alternative angles from which to reconstruct the country's past and give presence to marginalised groups (Valente, 1993: 41-2). The literary efforts involve a vision of enlarging Brazilian history from the monological state sponsored myth of the heritage of innate cultural benevolence and syncreticism, to expose the reality in the Brazilian past of institutionalised violence, persecution, and torture. Furthermore, their writings promote the emergence of a heteroglossic history that does not conceal the undesired self-images or, for the sake of national unity, avoid recognising and dealing with the complexity of the Brazilian cultural reality. As Valente puts it, Brazilian novels aim at redefining the collective past and present of Brazil, not to contest the notion of Brazil as a single nation state, but to counter official homogenising narratives with a recognition of the heterogeneity and plurality that paradoxically constitute "Brazilianness" (53-4).

Many South Africans have a history of being misrepresented or obliterated by institutionalised histories and, being denied the access to participate in the making of institutionalised histories, literature has often assumed the function of being an aperture for self-expression and self-assertion. In the course of the apartheid years, the reach between art, politics and historiography was remarkably narrowed as the arts changed into a territory of protest and counter-histories. The themes of writing were preoccupied with recording the circumstances of oppression that unfolded throughout the decades with the double objective of inciting domestic and international opposition against the apartheid system and documenting the aspects of the national narrative that were silenced in the official record. Earlier literary histories such as Sol Plaatjie's *Mhudi* (1930) countering the self-righteous historiography of Afrikaaner nationalism and Thomas Mofolo and R.R.R. Dhlomo's reclaims of the history of the Zulu kingdom were succeeded by apartheid writers, such as Alex la Guma,

Dennis Brutus, Lewis Nkosi, Richard Rive, Ezekiel Mphahlele, Can Themba, Mongane Wally Serote, Miriam Tlali, Sipho Sepamla and many more, who sought to seize the history of apartheid as it passed and represent it from a black perspective.

Correspondingly, the arts were deliberately incorporated in the resistance movement as a weapon against oppression. In the 1980s, the UDF defined the role and the direction of literature in the struggle against white minority rule. The performances and responsibilities of literature as envisioned by the UDF were unequivocal and determinably converged with the organisation's overall endeavours of mass mobilisation. The UDF included in their "people's culture" campaign a list of conditions on art that insisted that artists, the "cultural workers", submit their work to the discipline of a formal alliance with the UDF by making itself accessible to the "underclasses", building a national culture of unity among the oppressed groups, and heeding the emphasis on a concrete, documentary form of realism that precisely depicted the life-experience of the oppressed (Attwell, 1990: 101-2).

Literature lends itself generously to purposes of opposing the establishment. According to Jackson, it is possible to identify artistic modes of discourse as discourses of inherent resistance. Reason and administrative order, he argues, get associated with scientific facts, while emotionality and license get linked to fiction. Hence "the arts are critical of the sciences, folktales are satires on the myths of rulers and both are barely tolerated, and in [the west] underfunded. Factuality is friendly to administrative control while fiction threatens it" (Jackson, 2002: 93-4). The imaginative freedom of fiction allows it to be ontologically and epistemologically border breaking. As opposed to discourses that seek to establish fixed borders of inclusion and exclusion, literature may be employed to break the formal codes of truth and reality and thus to re-imagine and reset the terms of the community.

Referring to Gerd Baumann's terms of "dominant" and "demotic" discourses and Michael Herzfeld's notion of discursive disemia, Jackson points out the difference between the politics of storytelling in the public and the private domains respectively. The contrast is between the official truth and the unofficial indictment against that truth. As Herzfeld points out, the two discourses often use the same symbols, images and lexical forms, but they employ these for entirely different ends. The public discourse is spun from the objective of formal self-representation and as such the rhetoric of official discourse contends to be national, pure and consistent, defining fixed borders of reality, ushering absolute morality while of course denying its own rhetoricity. The demotic discourse, the unofficial, private politics of storytelling, defines itself in contrast to the official. Private storytelling hosts the privacy of collective introspection which, conscious of imperfection, constantly erodes the certainties of the idealistic certainties of the official discourse, replacing ideas of the national and the eternal with ideas of the immediate and the local, transgressing the borders of established truth and inverting the codes of meaning (Jackson, 2002: 17-8 and Herzfeld, 1987: 133, 135). As Jackson sums it up with an eye to the distinction between the official discourses of law, science, and objectivity and the private discourse of fiction and subjectivity:

> At the same time that the ancestral legacy of 'true' narratives lays down the law, reinforces respect for received values, and draws attention to the foundational principles of the social order, 'fictional' narratives persistently address quotidian problems of injustice, revealing the frailty of authority, mocking the foibles of men, and shaming all those who mask their greed and ambition with the language of ideology and the trappings of high office. And while some stories create and sustain dehumanising divisions between the powerful and the powerless – as in nationalist myths and fascist propaganda – others work to deconstruct such divisions and redress such imbalances, enabling the powerless to recover a sense of their own will, their own agency, their own consciousness, and their own being (Jackson, 2002: 27).

For these reasons, it is regretful that the past as recorded and challenged in the creative genres is commonly overlooked or even rejected in studies of the writings and constructions of history and national narratives. We are accustomed to regarding storytelling as less relevant, less precise, less reliable, less rational, less objective than non-literary forms of expression in questions of writing history. Literary storytelling, says Jackson, is usually marginalised "to the private domain, [as] a modality of leisure, a discourse of the uneducated, an artefact of childhood", while the historian has achieved an almost axiomatic monopoly and privilege in representing the truth of the past (Jackson, 2002: 94).

Yet, the recognition of literature as a valid medium in concerns of recording and giving shape to history has obtained support in recent years' deconstruction of history as a discourse. The conventional distinctions between different modes of rendering the past, between story and history, fiction and non-fiction have been radically reassessed and consequently blurred. On the one hand, light has been shed on the often neglected fact that the creative discourses play a significant role in the formation of historical awareness. It may be observed, for instance, that our "knowledge" of the past is shaped to a large degree by artful renditions such as monuments, paintings, historical plays and novels, as well as by T.V. drama series of historical eras and the inescapable show "based on a true story". Secondly, the idea of a clear-cut distinction between presenting *history* and telling a *story* and the indiscriminate elevation of factual discourses as non-textual have been problematised by studies of the methodological construction of non-literary discourses. As argued by Lars Ole Sauerberg, there are no differences between the historian's and the realist novelist's textual capturing of their object of study. Both kinds of writing make use of centralised events, order and coherency of existence, plots, flashbacks, anticipations, explorations of causes, climaxes, anti-climaxes, etceteras, the historian being no less interested in creating a "good read" (Sauerberg, 2001: 88, 90, 96-7). Sauerberg's observations rest on Hayden White's influential studies into the narrative core of historiography. White points to the fact that the writing of history cannot evade its dependence on narrative and analysis. Without narration and analysis, history would be as trivial as the recitation of singular events and their dates without further interest in the details of how and why. Added to this, White draws attention to the inconsistency in the historian's assumption that it should be possible to "let things speak for themselves" as all narratives are representational forms and as such determinedly attached to value markers such as perspective, selection, omission, voice and metaphor (White, 1987: 1-6, 24-5).

Questioning the qualitative demarcation between *history* and *story* is not an act of discrediting non-literary discourses, but an act of recognising literary discourses as valid and important ways of representing and giving voice to the past. Evidently this perspective is particularly imperative in the study of counter-histories among marginalised and oppressed groups. No discursive form can be rated as insignificant by a monopolised, conventionalised master discourse; rather, the alleyways to the past are open to be reached through a heterogeneity of form. But above all, the heightened awareness of the intentional disposition and the imagined and narrated content of any rendition of the past has deprived all modes of representation of the powerfully manipulative illusion of pretending to be analogous with reality. In other words, when all representations of the past have been de-established as metonymical truths and re-established as texts, relating to reality via deliberate methods of signification and symbolism, no representation of the past, fictional or factional, can be forwarded as untouchable by criticism and alternative perspectives.

This also means that literature does not necessarily comprise a "truer" gateway to the past than conventional history. Like any other representation of the past, literary renditions are not to be applauded as *passive* reflections of historical events and must be read critically like all meaning-making systems. Literature may expand the collective memory and responsibility, by casting light on repressed events, giving voice to the marginalised, the silenced, the forgotten; it may complicate any given national narrative by creating discontinuity and fragmentation, acknowledging a heritage of difference and defending the right to non-conformity; or it may counter imagined national ideals by voicing national acts of shame. But literature is far from exempt from endorsing fixed power structures. Absolutes may be established by screening out anything that questions existing ideology and it may contribute in projects that establish borders of exclusion, sustaining the antithetic logic of either or, and regimenting symbolic truth markers of black and white, purity and impurity. Literature has, for example, often been employed as a handmaiden of autocratic regimes in creating a national consciousness or collective divisions that support the issued political structure.

In South Africa, Sarah Gertrude Millin represents the prime example of a novelist who has used her writings of the past to justify and offer cultural support of state policies during the apartheid era. In her novel *King of the Bastards* portraying historical characters on the Eastern Cape frontier of late 18$^{th}$ and early 19$^{th}$ centuries, the cradle of Afrikaner nationalism, she dramatises the tragic consequences of miscegenation and any transgression of racial boundaries. Michael Green, who will provide the theoretical framework of this study, observes in Millin a method of representing racial distinctions and racism, not as products of historical circumstance, but as a transhistorical heritage, as innate human characteristics that are not to be explained or questioned but simply to be accepted (Green, 1997: 99). In this way, says Green, Millin reads a fully developed apartheid mentality of the mid-twentieth century into the past of the Eastern Cape frontier and, as a double strategy, she then proceeds to find the origin of that mentality in the past (128).

Similarly, many writings of the opposite camp that serve the purposes of counter-histories inevitably create their own biased versions of the collective narrative. In breathing life into antithetic realities, the most efficient method of stirring people, they generally engage in simplifying the differences between the excluded and the included, the right and the wrong, at the expense of pluralism, inconsistency and ambiguity. Certain sides to an incident may be exaggerated while others are being equally downplayed. Perpetration and questionable acts committed by one's own ranks, for instance, may be silenced completely by censorship or manipulated to appear as acts of justice and morality. At length, resistance rhetoric may contribute to the shaping and maintenance of an imagination of polarised absolutes and group oppositions, entrenching social imagination along automated codes of unthinking loyalty. Much literature of the struggle in South Africa is teeming with the dichotomising codes of *us* against *them*. With few exceptions, and altering between the portrayal of passive victimisation and active resistance, it is marked by martyrdom and heroism. It is contentious and confrontational and customarily based on simple moral premises of black virtue versus white evil. However imperative and necessary such literature is in the heat of the struggle, it has to be re-evaluated after the struggle according to the requirements and needs of new political and social contexts.

When a power vacuum emerges to be filled by a new political order in the wake of an oppressive regime or a civil war, the question is how the histories of the past and particularly the past uses of history for confrontational purposes are going to be employed in the creation of the country's new national narrative. Will the oppositional factions of the past be allowed to continue their dictation of the present and so to define the society of the future, allegorising the smallest acts into the hyperbolic political symbolism of *us* against *them* and *this idea* against *that*? Will ethnic, racial or other group formations within the nation be exploited to legitimise new exclusive politics and contentions for power and special privilege? Or will the dichotomising counter-history of the struggle emerge as a new state myth that legitimises a new, inverted form of group oppression? In sum, what kind of present and future politics is the past going to serve?

The crucial problem of the democratic transition in South Africa is one of making a post-apartheid imagination possible. History has been thwarted and retarded by the binary and polarised social imagination that has evolved and been consolidated over the decades since the 1950s. Hence, the present task of resuscitating, rewriting, and unwriting the past, of retelling and reorganising the country's historical narrative, becomes crucial in thawing the social controls and the binary emphasis that slide over into post-apartheid South Africa. In order to make the future possible at all, the new representations and interpretations of South African history must make it possible to transcend the dichotomies of the past by allowing social imagination to move beyond entrenched thinking of difference and separation.

But the task of re-writing history in South Africa since the fall of apartheid involves more than transcending the conditioning narratives of hostility and bigotry. There is an interconnected, meta-narrative challenge of finding new ways of representing and using the past that radically depart from the recurrent exploitation of history in schemes of oppression. The new engagement with history cannot continue the practise of making the past oblige to the present and using the past to endorse present ideologies. Rather, history must be set to work within a mode that eschews the conscious practise and the unconscious habit of shaping the past to the appeals of the present, whereby any engagement with history turns into a matter of challenging the status quo and questioning the adequacy of customary perceptions of reality. In other words, in order to prevent the repetition of past wrongs, the role of social, cultural and political opinion makers is to consciously situate themselves against the repetition of past exploitations of history.

In this context, literature, in its primary and unique capacity, identified by Jackson, as a medium of discursive transgression, may prove itself efficient. As a discursive and imaginatively free space where the borders of habitual thinking can be suspended, literature may inspire a shift in discursive "truth effects" from serving and conserving existing borders in the collective imagination to keep challenging these borders. The terms of discourse will then be other than binding meaning to antagonistic epistemologies. Discourses will be subjected to the terms of an episteme of shifting, nomadic dynamics, renewing themselves endlessly. The restrained energy of a discourse like history will then be released and the past liberated from its role of serving static ideas and fixed borders. Consequently, collective imaginations are never allowed to settle in established power relations said to be sacrosanct, ancestral and true. Rather, collective imaginations will be continuously informed and shaped by the volatility of shifting relations of power. In this way, history may be taken out of the control of the rulers, the victors, the privileged, and, instead of being used in collaboration with the status quo, be turned into a point of contention from which political power may be critically challenged at all times.

In present day South Africa, the discursive oppositions of the past linger on and society remains to a great extent racially charged. Among other things this is expressed in the accusations of racism, both black and white, that are frequently mud-slung through the public room. Says Dorothy Driver: "despite the death of apartheid…the social dynamic is still surprisingly often registered of 'black' and 'white'" (Driver, 1997: 100).

The heavy burden of the country's history and the strength of its divisions of thought in post-apartheid South Africa is expressed in J. M. Coetzee's much celebrated novel *Disgrace*. One of the dialogues between the main characters of the novel, David Lurie and his daughter Lucy, draws a terrifying relation between the burden of history and individual responsibility in the present when David interprets the rape of his daughter as an act of racial retribution. Lucy refers to the privacy of the incident: "'It was so personal', she says, 'It was done with such personal hatred. That was what stunned me more than anything. The rest was…expected. But why did they hate me so? I had never set eyes on them'" (Coetzee, 1999: 156). The idea of personal motives behind the crime is refused immediately by her father in perhaps the most central phrase of the book: "'*It was history speaking through them*…. A history of wrong. Think of it that way, if it helps. It may have seemed personal, but it wasn't. It came down from the ancestors'" (156, italics added).

Despite these obvious and socially impeding legacies of the past and despite the enormous enterprise of the Truth and Reconciliation Commission of mapping the details and complexities of apartheid history, the public discourse has been marked by a noticeable culture of amnesia. In the media of commercials, the past, as Eve Bertelsen put it, is typically reduced to just that…past. A 1994 ad showing the picture of a tilted milk carton, spilling a huge white (election) cross reads: "Why cry over spilt milk, when we can build a healthy nation" (Bertelsen, 1998: 226-7).

Often the culture of amnesia is politically motivated. Under the pretence of being more concerned with the future than with dwelling on the bygones, some voices disapprove of digging more dirt up from the past. This goes for F. W. De Klerk who already minted the term the "New South Africa" in his February 2 speech when proclaiming the end of apartheid in 1990. Undoubtedly, his intention was to narrate the future as severed from the past and his own party as the reincarnated righteous party, playing a crucial role in instituting a better South Africa (Attridge and Jolly, 1998: 5). Likewise, there has been a typical tendency to disregard the past in the publishing industry, for example. In anticipation of the new dawn, South African publishers of literature were preoccupied in the first half of the 1990s with the celebration of a break with the past, releasing anthologies that would supposedly capture the New South African fictional strands, the "post-apartheid spirit" (Driver, 1994: 131).

However, the assumed break with the past in public discourse is paralleled by serious attempts to interrogate the past in order to make sense of it and use it for various purposes in dealing with present problems. Among other forms of communication, and in spite of publishers' preoccupation with the exploration of new literary themes, it is acknowledged in much post-apartheid literature that the present cannot be severed from the past and the fact that the aftermath of apartheid stretches far into the present needs to be addressed.

The literary interrogation of South African history takes all kinds of forms, all in one way or another taking a stance towards the task of writing South African history and directing its future development. There are writers who reinvent the past in revisionist attempts to wriggle history from the distortions and lies created by white, male domination. Phyllis Ntantala's *A Life's Mosaic*, for instance, is about female upbringing in the 1940s and '50s; Jeanne Goosen's *Not All of*

*Us* explores lower middle-class Afrikaner family life in the same period; and Mandla Langa describes life in exile and ANC training camps in *The Naked Song*. There are attempts to fill the blank pages of history books with events that were silenced by the official records of history, as Ronnie Govender does in his depiction of the forced removal of an Indian community in *At the Edge and Other Cato Manor Stories*. Another literary reaction to the past is inspired by the postmodernist mission to undermine claims to objectivity, representation of reality and claim to narrative authority as in Chris van Wyk's *The Year of the Tapeworm* or André Brink's *Imaginings of Sand*. And Achmat Dangor in *Kafka's Curse* re-imagines South Africa and its complex identity problems through a revisit with the past that blends history with parable and dream.

The present study will present but three examples of ways in which South African writers engage with the country's recent history. This will be done through a presentation of historical themes in and a discussion of the related discursive possibilities and problems pertaining to three main works: Mongane Wally Serote's *Gods of Our Time*; Mike Nicol's *The Ibis Tapestry*; and Zakes Mda's *Ways of Dying*.

These novels have been chosen for their shared features as well as for their marked differences. All three look back on the final years of apartheid, the 1980s, with Zakes Mda's novel taking us into the years of transition before the first democratic elections. Moreover, all engage in the question of what usefulness the country's past may have for South Africa's present and future. Yet they constitute three diverse responses to the past.

*Gods of Our Time* is a realist exploration of the textures of life in the underground resistance movement. As such, the novel offers a portrayal of the "hidden people" of the struggle, the sacrifices of ordinary lives in the fight against oppression. In addition to the illustration of the organisational structures of the resistance, Serote supplements the hard facts of South African records of history with subjective experience under the strain of apartheid – the doubts and fears, heroism, cowardice, betrayal, frustration, etceteras. The subjective thrust of the novel is accompanied by a probe into the psychological scars that have been caused by the violence of the time and a suggestion of how art and creativity may ameliorate the pain. Yet, in spite of Serote's display of the suffering of the oppressed, the overall impression is not that of a passive victimised people. Stoicism and determination lend credence to Serote's deliberate intention of paying tribute to and asserting the agency of the people in the demise of apartheid. A final very important aspect that is prevalent in Serote's revisit with the past is his ability to complicate the general black and white picture of apartheid. By marking the presence of exceptions to the rule in our ideas of the era, in granting space for white solidarity to black resistance and recognizing the human rights violations committed in the name of liberation, Serote resists any possibility of a new totalisation of the country's history.

From the agents in the camp of resistance in *Gods of Our Time*, we move to the agents of oppression in *The Ibis Tapestry*. Mike Nicol's project is radically different from Serote's. With *The Ibis Tapestry*, he continues the post-structuralist approach to history that characterises much of his previous work. The novel is concerned with disclosing the textuality of history and with direct reference to the mandate of the Truth and Reconciliation Commission, he questions the accessibility of the "truth" and the "reality" of the past. Whereas Serote attempts to represent the reality of the past, like any other historian or any historical undertaking like the Truth and Reconciliation Commission, and thus to contribute to the pool of historical information with but a subjective account of lived experience, Nicol's bid is an intellectual assault against the master narrative of history in an effort to 'decolonise' the subordination of literature to history and assert the independence of literary discourse in dealing with historical topics. One possible result, as will be seen, is that history is represented as parody. Yet Nicol's problematisation of conventional history, truth, reality and his parodic experiments do not serve the purpose of historical denial. On the contrary, the deconstruction of history and the amplification of literature enable Nicol to exceed the kind of closure that is put on the past by historical discourse and summon in its stead a form of unease that appeals to everlasting remembrance and unrelenting culpability.

In terms of form, Zakes Mda's *Ways of Dying* may be read as an amalgamation of the other two approaches. By using the tradition in African oral culture of magical realism, Mda embarks on an application of history, which neither refuses representation of reality nor subordinates itself to the supposed supremacy of historical discourse in representing the past. Contentwise, we move from Serote's and Nicol's explorations into the agents of resistance and repression respectively to the marginalised sideline of the squatter camps where people are searching for ways of living within a brutalising history.

If Serote is engaged mainly with history as the past, or how the past should be represented in the present, and Nicol, in the sense of reacting directly to the Truth Commission and the current questions of guilt and atonement, is engaged with history as the present, Zakes Mda's novel presents a perception of history as the future in the sense that it implies two scenarios of post-apartheid South Africa. The country can move in the direction of either a utopia or a dystopia, all depending on its ability or willingness to relieve the majority of the people from ideological, cultural and material deprivation. Suitably, *Ways of Dying* is read in this context as a vision that adds to Serote's proposition of political empowerment a need for socio-cultural empowerment as well as Mda concretizes Nicol's abstract notions of guilt and contrition with a call for material reparation.

The study is thus informed by the three objectives of exemplifying the range of themes that are present in South African historical fiction and to explain the reasons for engaging with these themes; to exemplify the range of forms that are adopted to deal with these themes and discuss what possibilities and problems the choice of form entails; and, thirdly, to suggest the movement in South African literature towards a holistic conceptualisation of what history is, enveloping as historical time the past, the present and the future.

That leads us to the fourth and last objective of the study. As the analyses and discussions of the works progress, it will be examined how each of the writers manages to make use of the past as a critical investment in the present and the future, be it as an effort to heal the wounds of a traumatic past, to resist the dangers of a new totalitarian national history, to prevent the development of historical amnesia, to question the authority of the present, to address questions of guilt, atonement and national redistribution. This will be done mainly in the conclusion of each analysis by considering each work in relation to Michael Green's theory of "resistant form". In his comprehensive work on the nature of South African historical fiction, *Novel Histories*, Green stresses the importance that writers' thematisation of history should be sufficiently critical in order that their "histories" be capable of passing judgement on the present and the future. This, Green argues, may be accomplished by a balancing act between two poles of historical perception. On the one hand, there is an element of totalitarianism in seeing history as a continuous and connected process which may end in a domestication of the past in the form of knowing it. The historian or the novelist achieves disciplinarian control over the past and history becomes a product of the present, which in the worst case may lead to a use of the past as a justification of present power structures. On the other hand, there is the Foucaultian perception of emphasising "discontinuity" in history which demonstrates the foreignness, the strangeness and inaccessibility of the past that is necessary to relativize or undercut the legitimacy of the present. This approach, however, runs the risk of separating the past from the present to an extent that it erroneously loses its contemporary relevance.

The balancing act between the two poles, the resistant form, is the search for a use of history which is resistant to simply appropriating history to present purposes and yet relevant enough to relate meaningfully to the present. Or, in other words, it is a search for a way in which history, as past, present and future, may be read from the present without allowing it to endorse the policies of the present; it must represent a continual challenge to current historiographic, ideological, economic or political forces[4].

By examining the three novels as resistant forms, it is hoped that it will appear how a particular kind of South African historical literature, while concerned with disclosure and remembering, may be applied primarily to assess and to try the present of the new South Africa and its future and how this kind of writing positions itself against the manipulation of history by new totalitarian politics.

# Mongane Wally Serote: *Gods of Our Time*

*Gods of Our Time* is set in the 1980s in the dying days of apartheid. A brief historical glance at the period reveals an oppressive system that desperately tries to buttress itself against the foreign and domestic pressure that is striving to end it.

P. W. Botha was inaugurated as president in 1978 and his maxim of the world waging a "total onslaught" against the apartheid state was an expression of the austerity of the threats against the regime. Botha's administration was faced with a severe economic recession with soaring inflation rates; a population growth that outdid the growth of the GNP; a shortage of skilled labour due to an education plan that would forever keep other races less skilled than the white (Thompson, 1990: 221, 223-4). These hard facts made it extremely difficult to maintain the enormous bureaucracy required by a segregationist state. They also made the business of keeping insurgency and resistance at bay prohibitively costly, not to mention the money-draining policy of destabilising the neighbouring states (221, 224).

Internationally, the awareness of the South African system as an anomaly in the world was growing, despite the stubborn support of the National Party by Reagan, Thatcher and their likes (222, 223). Domestically, the Black Consciousness movement and the general anger aroused by the massacre in Soweto 1976 inspired a new wave of mass protest among blacks, coloureds and Indians, which was but extremised by the township youth in the 1980s (228).

Botha's response to the growing internal resistance and international pressure was a twofold attempt to appear reform-friendly while avoiding relinquishing white supremacy. First, the apartheid state was reformed on the surface by abolishing a number of inessential apartheid regulations, such as the Immorality Act, the Public Amenities Act, etc. In addition, the tricameral constitution was introduced, allowing a limited amount of representation in Parliament for coloureds and Indians, while still excluding blacks (224-5). Needless to say, these measures, and in particular the latter, had the very opposite effect of appeasing resistance. So the second spike of Botha's fork was to adopt increasingly harsh measures in suppressing opponents of the state. The State Security Council, comprising, among others, the Minister of Defence, Magnus Malan; the heads of the defence forces; police and intelligence; all under the leadership of the president, became stronger than the Cabinet – thus rendering the leadership of the country military rather than civil (224).

Apart from sending invading troops to Angola and Mozambique, the Security Council went out of its way domestically to instigate ethnic violence and class cleavages to undercut the strength of a unified resistance as well as to orchestrate the notorious Third Force activities, a special covert police unit with the mission of finding, torturing and liquidating any prominent anti-apartheid activist (224).

Like the removal of the mere symbols of apartheid, this only aggravated the situation in the country. It all came to a head in June 1986 when a three-year-long state of emergency was imposed. The police were invested with broad powers of arrest, detention, and interrogation, without a warrant, meetings were banned and the media were prohibited from covering any unrest. The government, as Leonard Thompson puts it, had resorted to legal tyranny (225).

The state of emergency had severe human repercussions. Incarcerations escalated with human rights violations and killing rates followed suit (236). A virtual war was taking place in the townships where the South African Defence Force had deployed five to eight thousand soldiers against a generation of youth that sought to "make the country ungovernable" (235).

It is in this macrocosm of desperate apartheid oppression against an increasing radicalisation of mass resistance that the events of Serote's novel unfold. The reader is supplied, in great detail, with images of the general picture of South Africa in the period. We are at a time when "Europeans Only" signs have been removed from benches while the violence of the clashes between the powers of oppression and its resistance is escalating. The familiar pictures of the army and police firing at hundreds and hundreds of youths throwing stones and Molotov cocktails are evoked throughout the novel. And so are the reminiscences of the political mass funerals, the necklacings, the stay-aways, the black trade union congresses and much more.

Yet Serote takes us beneath the surface images of the times and provides an insightful portrayal of the hidden people of the struggle at grass roots level. In this context, Serote's revisit with the past appears to carry two main objectives which will be examined in turn. Firstly, in a tribute to the common people who devoted themselves to the everyday struggle, Serote takes pains to assert the agency of the people in the demise of apartheid. This intention runs in accord with the personal conviction he has always had that "the strength of organised people cannot be defeated" (Moyo, 1990: 54) and positions itself against historical arguments that ascribe more importance to internal divisions within the Afrikaner camp and international pressures as factors that dissolved the unjust regime. Secondly, Serote, in close congruence with his focus on the people, is striving to convey a sense of lived experience in the resistance movement. In many ways this second ambition can be read as a late response to Njabulo Ndebele's appeal to South African literature to "...move away from an easy preoccupation with demonstrating the obvious existence of oppression". Literature, according to Ndebele, should rather explore how and why people could live under the harsh conditions of oppression: "Make life the material subject of our imaginative explorations". And "through a total evocation of [the lives of the oppressed] create an active philosophical interest in the complex dialectic of human existence" (Ndebele, 1994: 161). In regard of this literary plea, particularly, Serote's exploration of the widespread suffering from psychological strain will be examined, as it, too, has compelling relevance to the country's psychological make-up at present.

Moses Motsamayi, the I-narrator, in describing the vast anonymous number of people that comprise the collective resistance, poses a repetitive series of questions which the novel itself seeks to answer, or at least attempt to answer, by way of example, in order to crack open the surface of the sweeping terms like "resistance movement",

"Umkhonto we Sizwe", "UDF", etc. in history books, and reveal the ordinary people contained underneath:

> What is this force...? The crowd, the dots, the moving dots.... Who is the Movement? These dots? This crowd? People who are drowning must feel like this: space and space, substance and substance all around, but nowhere to hold on...who is the Movement? (73-4).

The impossibility of personalising the dizzying impersonality that makes up "the force", as well as telling its story, is recognised throughout by Moses who, to the very end, admits that "...the story of this time is not finished" and too many questions are left unanswered, suspended in darkness "like many ribbons" (281). Nevertheless, Serote imparts some idea of who these hidden people were, what their ideals were, their dreams, their determination and courage, their fears, doubts, frustrations, limits, pains, secrets. We are invited into the lives of several people engaged somehow or other in the resistance milieu in the township of Tembisa and other places of the Witwatersrand. There is the character of Lindi, the singer, who suffers from "combat fatigue", there are the stoic children who, despite their age, have assumed the responsibility of leadership, and function as judges of life and death. There is the henchman, Eddie, the agent Jacob, the disengaged Lucas who is accused of treachery, the white activist Barbie, and Moses who is in the armed wing of the ANC, Umkhonto we Sizwe.

The overall atmosphere in the underground world is described by Nomvula, a mother who resolved to dedicate her life to the cause for which her son sacrificed his life:

> It was after Sipho's death that she became aware of this world, the world of many people who came and went; who today one hears about, tomorrow one talks to, and then one day are gone; they may come back, they may not (108).

And it is a world of danger and constant unease. Not only is there the risk of being arrested, tortured, or shot by the secret police, there is also the unease and solitude of living under cover where not even the closest partner can be trusted:

> It meant at times you do not ask questions; it meant at times you do what you are told; it meant that you could expect, and it would be expected of you; it meant to trust and not to trust... (157).

However, despite the hardship, they carry on relentlessly, as Andries Oliphant puts it, upholding the self-preserving counter-action of the community against state terrorism (Oliphant, 1999: 18). At times, as in the case of Nomvula, participation in these self-preserving structures is the only salvation from despair. Joining the greater purpose of the movement and the preoccupation of the mind with practicalities help her overcome the loss of her son:

> Nomvula sensed that this world which she now found herself part of was spreading, she felt it was fathomless and endless like the sea. Every day she was learning new things, more than she had learnt in all the thirty-seven years of her life.... she had come to learn that...a world underneath the world existed (108-9).

The people that make up the covert world are organised in an informal, yet extremely efficient machine of resistance. Democratic meetings and ANC directions are the fountainheads of the activities that are carried out, encoded messages and orders are passed on orally with great expediency, strict codes of conduct are formulated and must be observed, a clear focus is maintained by a constant formulation of priorities and strategic intelligence and protection is secured through good relations with the local population.

When presented with the details of the actual organisation of the people in *Gods of Our Time*, it is very tempting in these times of historical recuperation in South Africa to claim that Serote's novel is one of the books that write out the empty pages of the country's history by disclosing hidden structures of the underground resistance. The cover blurb, for instance heralds the novel as filling "an important gap in South Africa's history" (Serote, 1999). However, a proposition like that appears to be rather overzealous when considering the substantial research in the struggle movement that was undertaken in the 1980s by the so-called "social history movement". Not unlike the thrust of Serote's novel, the mission of the social historians was to write "history from below" or "popular history" (Legassick and Minkley, 1998: 103-4). Even the personalisation of history is well-trodden ground as, to one of the movement's best known proponents Shula Marks, social history was concerned with a "picture alive with real people" and "personalising the workings of large historical forces" (Green, 1997: 14)[5]. In that respect, Serote's project can be seen as affiliated with the social history project, but the organisation of the resistance movement and portrayals of people involved have already been systematically investigated by such historians as Marks, Cobbet and Cohen as well as in the work of Anthony Marx (see bibliography).

But even if Serote's raw material is not new discovery, the documentary elements in the novel are of particular importance in regard to the politics of representation. Ranajit Guha was mentioned in the introduction in regard to the failure of Indian historiography in representing the subaltern, given social, epistemological and ideological distances between the professional historian and the Indian peasant. Similar discrepancies exist in South Africa between the institutionally established recorders of history and the actors within that history themselves. As Legassick and Minkley point out, academic historians in South Africa have always remained and continue to remain predominantly white and male (Legassick and Minkley, 1998: 99). Accordingly, academic historical writing has typically resulted in either of two outcomes. Either the failure to reflect critically on the implications of representing an Other, even among the social historians, effects a practice of paternalism towards black, Indian, coloured and female history or the academy retreats to safer grounds by "examining whiteness", thus evading completely the difficulties of representing the subaltern (106-7, 117). The latter, which has become the predominant tendency since the beginning of the 1990s, has engendered sharp criticism of professional history production from various sources in South Africa which blame the academe for not writing the history of the struggle (98, 104, 108). Guha criticises the Indian historians of the Nationalist school, and other schools of Indian historiography, of not acknowledging a political consciousness on behalf of the peasant rebels of anti-colonial insurrections in the previous two centuries. In South Africa, official histories are criticised of rating the domestic anti-apartheid struggle as a secondary factor in bringing down the apartheid state; of less importance than the presumed effects of international sanctions and diminishing support for discriminatory laws within the white population and governing bodies.

In accordance with the critique of the predominantly white academe, it can be observed in Leonard Thompson's *A History of South Africa*, which was quoted at the beginning of this chapter and which is one of the most popular general histories of South Africa, how the domestic struggle has been granted much less space than other factors. At the risk of sounding fastidiously calculative, attention should be drawn to the fact that the chapter on "Apartheid in Crisis 1976-1986" devotes two pages to the struggle, whereas the account of government policy, internal dialectics in the Afrikaner community, macroeconomics and foreign sanctions take up nineteen pages (Thompson, 1990: 221-242).

In that light, Serote continues the tradition developed among non-white and female writers of countering "official" history production in South Africa by documenting their own history in the creative genres of literature, in autobiography, as well as in journalism and photography. At the same time, he escapes the ramifications of representation that have incapacitated white historians with the additional quality that he has had first-hand experience with the underground environment from his time as an MK soldier (Solberg, 1998: 180).

By using his historical point of departure to assert the people as the prime agent in changing the country, Serote offers a much needed critical response to the many proclamations that apartheid ended primarily because of the pressure of economic sanctions imposed by the international community and internal divisions in the white camp with capitalist and academic interests ranged against worker interests. This is done, on the one hand, through the overall presentation of the resistance as a highly organised structure peopled by activists of great dedication to their cause, and, on the other hand, with direct reference to the crucial blows which were being dealt repeatedly to the system by the people. As an example, Moses addresses the important role played by the black trade unions in paralysing the country's economy:

> "…the hand of the workers was reaching for the balls of the white giant. The giant knew this. The giant could no longer go on as if it did not feel its balls being squeezed. It felt the grip, the slow tightening. It was lashing out, at times blindly, at times in anticipation of the next squeeze, the next grip" (169).

And at another time, the strength of the movement is affirmed despite the claims of its opponents and critics:

> "I don't see what the newspapers say. I see, I feel a force stronger than any steel or diamond. It is unleashed, and I hear America, Britain, and France, and I think, how come they don't know that it will crush every thing before it? Why? (99).

What is moreover implied in the latter extract, apart from the uncrushable force of the people, is a devaluation of the importance of international pressure. Throughout the novel it is stressed that the role of international sanctions in ending apartheid is highly questionable given the lack of political will and integrity that characterised the, at that time, conservative politics of the West. In fact, the international community assisted the apartheid regime, with loans and through trade, well into the latter half of the 1980s. As it is coined at a funeral speech:

> Young men and women die like flies before a frightened and ruthless lot who are armed and paid by Reagan and Thatcher and the western countries (30).

In like manner, Serote breaks new ground for history writing by giving special prominence to women who, typically, it might be added, have not been accorded the recognition they deserve for their involvement in the fight against apartheid (see Russell, 1989: 23)[6]. In fact, the movement Serote describes is in many instances held together or enforced by a remarkably strong and energetic female presence, which, traditionally, used to be no more than "the function and silence of the furniture in a house" (64). Now women have raised themselves against male predominance to perform key roles in the struggle. Not only are they organised in special women's committees which take care of crucial tasks such as counselling, mobilisation of the masses and fundraising, they participate, too, on an equal footing, in central decision-making and in the actual fights on the streets (36-7, 65-9). There are also a number of women who join the armed wing of the ANC, Umkontho we Sizwe. Among them are Moses' wife, Esther, the shop owner's daughter, Rebekka, but also the white activist Barbie who risks her life as the central figure in the selection and testing of new recruits for the MK (267, 198, 142 and 182).

In particular the girl Cynthia emerges as the narration progresses as a heroic fighter who toughens both in the clashes with the police and in the hard environment of her group (14, 77-9 and 237-40). This earns her the entrusted responsibility, at a very young age, of creating new bases for resistance outside Tembisa (105). From her experiences, Cynthia also develops a determined awareness of gender equality. In a discussion with her sixty-year-old friend, Tholo, she demands that he re-evaluate his old-fashioned view of women: "Rhe-Tholo, the Movement says there is no difference between men and women – what difference there is, is caused by society, and we want to correct that!" (59).

With the prominent role Serote grants to the people in bringing about the changes of South Africa, as well as the credit he grants female activists in the same breath, the past is used as an affirmation set against the history production of the academic establishment. Yet this affirmation is not entirely devoid of self-criticism.

Paul Russell once said, "if truth is the main casualty of war, ambiguity is another...[as] one of the legacies of war is a habit of simple distinction, simplification and opposition...which continues to do much of our thinking for us" (Krog, 1999: 150). The simple dichotomy in South Africa before 1990, seen from the perspective of the oppressed, was that of black righteousness and decency against the moral depravity of whites. However, as opposed to the tradition of realist depiction of the oppression from which he emerges, Serote reaches beyond the old polarised picture of South African society.

Rather than a self-glorified depiction of a victorious black population, Serote includes topics that prevent an unblemished depiction of resistance activities. If the human rights violations of the Third Force on their notorious death farms have any counterpart among crimes committed in the name of liberation, it has to be the so-called necklacings which were public executions of alleged traitors by burning[7]. Serote himself has condemned necklacings as "one of the saddest moments of the South African struggle" (Solberg, 1998: 184) and in *Gods of Our Time* the controversy is spelled out in the execution of the shop owner, Lucas.

Although on the surface Lucas appears unsympathetic to the struggle by associating with the police and declaring neutrality and might be unwittingly responsible for the police murders of six children, his situation is much more problematic than perceived by the youth of the movement. His private life is torn between two poles, fearing the intimidating warnings by the police to cut all connections with the movement and, on the other side, the youth who suspect him of being an informer (111-2). To fully back up either side would, no doubt, entail a fatal outcome. Above all, he wants to be left alone by everyone to take care of his business and his family as a loving father and husband. He is disgusted by the violence of the township whether committed by the police or by the anti-apartheid groups (111).

The hearings of the Truth Commission abound in cases of people who were executed for petty reasons in the name of liberation, indicating that the practice of necklacing was an outburst of barbarism rather than a strategic and necessary evil. In 1985 the first person to be necklaced, for instance, had only failed to observe a consumer boycott (Krog, 1999: 203). The ANC in their submission to the Commission continually stressed that their war, and hence their methods, were just. Necklacing, it was also claimed, was never part of official policy (158). Countering this attempt to institute a new warped national script, Sindiwe Magona, in her novel *Mother to Mother*, argues that: "Not many of our leaders came out and actually condemned the deed. Indeed, there were those who actually applauded the method.... They said it would lead us to freedom" (77)[8].

Serote, in his endeavour to problematise the issue, is less straightforward than Magona, but at the end of the day equally regretful. In *Gods of Our Time* two forces seem to be at work in the movement. On the one hand, there is the considerate and the strategic, like the older Mlambo and MaNhlabo, who regret the use of necklacing and argue that the allegiance of people like Lucas should be won by persuasion. On the other hand, there is the much stronger destructive force of rash, bloodthirsty youth who have been corrupted by the power they hold over life and death mixed with anger and apathy (39-41). Eventually, it is the latter force that fails or refuses to understand the complexity of Lucas' situation and kills him in complete disregard of the appeals of the more considerate (116). What Serote seems to infer in this description of the movement is the fact that the leadership of the UDF lost control to the youth during the 1980s. By

1985 about five thousand people had been detained without trial, leaving the resistance leaderless. As Krog says:

> Thousands of destabilised and leaderless youths saw themselves as the soldiers of the struggle. But they soon became gangs, roaming the streets and meting out their own version of justice. They became personal fiefdoms and small power bases using extreme forms of punishment (Krog, 1999: 381).

This explains, to some extent, how things got out of hand in the struggle and a phenomenon like necklacing was allowed to develop. Nevertheless, the "gods" in the novel are not infallible gods and Serote acknowledges the suffering caused by the liberation movement in spite of the ANC's claim to a just cause.

At the other end of the equation, Serote invites a corresponding breach in the oppositional logic of the warring times. The picture of the evil white is maintained in the character of the death squad leader Derek van Niekerk who roams the township on the lookout for the enemy of the state. The character of van Niekerk seems to be cut on some of the most notorious apartheid henchmen, like Eugene de Kock and Dirk Coetzee, who revealed their culpability in one of the darkest chapters of South African history at the Truth Commission's hearings (see Krog, 1999: 90-104). Indeed the detailed account of van Niekerk's systematic, almost scientific, methods of torture and subsequent execution of the ANC comrade, Eddie, echo the most sickening accounts from the death farms that formed a central part of Botha's and de Klerk's Third Force operations (Serote, 1999: 123-8). The chilly baseness of the affair is drawn full circle when van Niekerk, after executing such inexplicable cruelty, returns home to relax with his wife as if after an ordinary day at an ordinary job (128). However, the simplified portrayal of whites as pure evil that served the purpose of mobilising resistance in the struggle literature is counterweighed by the humanity of van Niekerk's wife who finds herself unable to stay with her husband when she discovers what cruelty he is capable of (247). Similarly Barbie's involvement in the

ANC and other examples of white support of the struggle, although not cleansing all white South Africans, does recognise the picture of the past as more than black and white.

Ingrid de Kok has posed the question whether the epistemological simplification in war that Paul Russell refers to will continue to govern the perceptions of the past in post-apartheid South Africa:

> Can an iconography of memory develop that will advance complexity and variety and mediate between the discourses of the past and the present self? Or will the literary project produce another binary system to secure a rigid, authorized public version of the past and the present? (8).

Serote's novel certainly shows, as do many other contemporary works, that the "literary project" is more likely to complicate the past than to freeze it in old dichotomies. And in that very willingness to acknowledge complexity and ambiguity lies, perhaps, the greatest foundation for reaching a reconciliatory understanding across the divisions of the South African society.

As mentioned, Serote's novel may be seen as a continuation of the practice among black South African writers of recording history in the genre of literature. Benita Parry explains how this practice was encoded into an austere set of conventions that adhered to the political objectives of the struggle:

> The preference for a responsible realism aimed at reclaiming black history and registering black agency was reinforced on different grounds by 'cultural agendas' devised during the 1980s by the most visible organisations of the liberation movement. These decreed that writers commit themselves to developing a purposeful, expressive, and accessible literature depicting oppression, [and] illuminating the struggle (Parry, 1998: 160).

The result of such a pragmatic protocol for literary creativity was, in addition to a "solidarity criticism" (finger-pointing any challenging diversions, such as Coetzee's use of ambiguity and irony, while praising any prodigal content regardless of the formal quality), a widespread preoccupation with a rather trite and superficial form of realism (for "solidarity criticism" see Sachs, 1998: 239). As Njabulo Ndebele points out, the mechanical debasement of the unjust system in the mode of accurate reportage resulted in:

> ...very little transformation in reader consciousness...since the only faculty engaged is the faculty of recognition. Recognition does not necessarily lead to transformation: it simply confirms (Ndebele, 1994: 31).

Art, then, becomes a matter of "informing without involving" (29). Against that backdrop, an awareness has long been under way that there is an urgent need to redefine the autonomy and the commitment of the arts in South Africa (Parry, 1998: 160). The change, it is arguable, is also visible in *Gods of Our Time* in that Serote seems bent on pushing the confines of the South African realist tradition of protest that constitutes his medium. Firstly, in terms of content, it has been illustrated that the novel transcends the old epistemology "...in which reality is conceived purely in terms of a total polarity of absolutes" (Ndebele, 1994: 60) by allowing considerable white involvement in the struggle and by acknowledging the indefensible human rights violations committed in the name of liberation. Secondly, Serote also exceeds the old realist doctrines by refusing a mere reportage of historical documentation. This he does in an attempt to penetrate the psyche of a traumatised society in a portrayal of the mental scars that have been caused by a life mercilessly entrapped in violence and denigration. In Jackson's terms, as cited in the introduction, Serote analyses the human consequences of being completely overpowered and objectified by forces outside one's own control. The main metaphor he deploys in this respect is that of an unsettling silence that haunts the text with its all-pervading presence.

The psychological character of the silence is continually stressed by its presence amidst the noise of traffic, shooting, shouting or dogs barking. Moses observes:

> There is a silence here. It is a silence which will not be broken by the roaring cars, the shattered glass, the deafening and deadly sound of the rifle – it is a silence as still as a tree when there is no wind blowing. But since we discovered this silence it is no longer there, it is now too loud (9).

As the passage suggests the awareness of the silence, once it is discovered, is unbearable. It screams and roars to be addressed. Yet addressing it appears to be a next to impossible task since its causes have also eroded the means to cure it, which is realised by Moses at a much later point:

> This present we were living had, without our being aware, erased our survival vocabulary, and burnt into our tongues a language which Lindi and I, seated on this red park bench with its erased 'Europeans Only' sign, were consciously trying to articulate. If we did articulate it, we would have to become new friends, living in a new time (97)

The absence of a "survival language", a language with which to cope with the naked terror which is mercilessly racing through each individual life, a language with which to imbue the absolute senselessness of the moment when a child is shot with some kind of ameliorating meaning or purpose, makes itself felt again and again. Silence is the only response that is left when Nomvula covers the corpse of her son prostrated at the feet of two policemen and silence is all that meets Cynthia when she brings news of another child's death (15 and 17). The capitulation to silence at such moments of intense grief evokes a sense of clogged emotional response, the sign of a psychological defence system so callused that it has arrested the outlet of natural reactions like moaning or anger.

However, there are times when the spell of the silence is broken. The most significant of these moments are when artistic creativity exposes the silence for people to realise its presence. This is what Lindi manages at one point with her song:

> The voice, Lindi's voice – this is what it said when it carried the words of the song, the harmony, the melody and the rhythm of the silence of the words: it was clasping the silence, the vast, the large, the heavy, deep silence of the sky..." (63).

Once the silence has been projected, creativity may begin to work it, but not by lamenting or regretting losses. At a rehearsal for a song, Lindi tries to make her band find the right tune for a song for South African children – using the example of Hector Peterson who was the first child to be shot in Soweto 1976. Rather than pity, she wants the musicians to hit a note of tributary love and embrace. She wants to capture the scene of Hector entering the street with a warm celebration of necessity and explains to the piano:

> ...he is about to go out into the street, to march, to demonstrate, you cannot stop him...because you yourself have come to know that it is important that he go to the street to march. We, you, all of us know there is a fire there. He must go through it. We cannot waste time by crying. We must know how to love him; can you make that out of the piano? Please, John, we must love Hector, hey, John, please man..." (96-7).

This is of course a turn of perception that is hard to come by to musicians whose lives, like the rest of society, are permeated by the constrained pain of loss. The session ends with "a terrible silence in the torn room" (47). However, at the end of the novel Lindi's message appears to achieve some kind of a break-through. She succeeds in mirroring the silence of the audience in a night club. As captured by Moses:

> There is something stunning about a voice which hangs like a cloud, like smoke, like a rainbow, like the stars or the moon itself, hanging, holding on – it is stunning when it does this in a space filled with people who are silent, who lean back in their chairs or hold on to each other, in each other's arms in a dark room.... The people, in their melancholic poses, forming silhouettes against the voice and against the darkness and the light...." (279).

The locus of Moses' description is the sound. It punctures the silence with transcendence, hanging "like a cloud", "like a rainbow", "like the stars". It is as if the music functions as a trope for expressing that inexpressible perseverance of hope, "holding on", that has to exist untouched by and in counterbalance to the sordid reality that produces the silence.

In comparison to the effect of the sound, the lyrics may seem less significant. Notwithstanding, it may be argued that the words of Lindi's song accompany the connotations of the sound with a sense of dignified purpose that otherwise seems lost in the meaninglessness of violence. We are asked why we are sending Themba on the road to Umtata when the road is bad and wrought with hazards like ditches, witches and crocodiles. The answer is in the imperative: he *has* to go and he *is* going to Umtata (279-81). Umtata, the capital of the former homeland of Transkei, derives its name from the river Mta. "Mta" in Xhosa means "the seizer", a name given the river after a number of people drowned in it, or the "river of the dead", from the custom of ceremoniously casting the dead into it (Raper, 1987: 230). As in the case of Hector Peterson, it has become the fate of the young to cross dangers and finally plunge themselves into death. But rather than mourning the sad loss, they should be sent off with the respect and ceremony of heroes, in celebration of their courage and sacrifice.

At one point, Ndebele requested that writers of protest literature "...get rid of the obsession with the white other [to] explore the self-sufficient psychology of the oppressed" (73). Congruently, the vision of oppression in Lindi's song has been completely internalised to the community of the oppressed. The white agent of injustice and malignancy is obscured by the symbolic "ditches", "witches" and "crocodiles", all of which renders suffering and death much less a loss at the hand of the white man than a fatalistic and beneficial sacrifice for the communal good. Lindi's insistence on a warm tribute to the dead and the dying at the expense of pity is complete. The same can be said about Serote's narration as a whole which itself exposes the silence, or the causes of the pain, and works on it creatively afterwards to effect some relief. Certainly, the novel succeeds, in Ndebele's terms, in moving beyond the stage of merely activating the reader's faculty of recognition and engages the reader in a transition of consciousness. As with Lindi's song, the reader is encouraged, with the novel, to experience a change of perception from regretting the human losses of the past to appreciating the courage with which the inevitable fate is met. This emotional exorcisation through creativity is a near-perfect coinage of André Brink's idea of literature as having an almost therapeutic role in post-apartheid South Africa:

> Historians (like psychiatrists) seek to refamiliarize us with events which have been forgotten [in this case the entrapment of emotion in a cul de sac compunction] through either accident, neglect or repression. Whether this occurs in therapy, in historiography, or in literature, the powerful act of appropriating the past through imaginative understanding – that is through the devices of metaphor rather than 'scientific objectivity' which tries to mask its own uncertainties – is necessary for the sanity of the whole community" (Brink, 1996: 23).

However, it should be noted that the creativity in this context does not involve a complete escape from the pain of the past. Its cultural reworking prevents, as Brink indicates, an unhealthy inhibition, which does not lead to catharsis but to an *acceptance* of the past as it was. Serote's novel, in this perspective, is an attempt through artistic creativity to reach an understanding of the senselessness of loss in the violent clashes of the 1980s. The lesson is one of transcending the paralysis of thought caused by pain; to open the mind to affirmative interpretations, to an acceptance, of the scars of the past. In Jackson's words:

> Storytelling is usually prompted by some crisis, stalemate, or loss of ground in a person's relationship with others and with the world, such that autonomy is undermined. Storytelling is a coping strategy that involves making words stand for the world, and then, by manipulating them, changing one's *experience* of the world. By constructing, relating and sharing stories, people continue to restore viability to their relationship with others, redressing bias towards autonomy when it has been lost, and affirming collective ideals in the face of disparate experiences. It is not that speech is a replacement for action, rather it is a supplement to be exploited when action is impossible or confounded [....] What matters is how stories enable us to regain some purchase over the events that confound us, humble us, and leave us helpless, salvaging a sense that we have some say in the way of our lives unfold. In telling a story we renew our faith that the world is within our grasp (Jackson, 2002: 8 and 7).

This is an intention of art that seems to be communicated in much creative writing in post-apartheid South Africa, and we shall return to it in both Mike Nicol and Zakes Mda. In this regard, it might also be added that the tentative approval of a self-sufficient taxonomy in Lindi's song, which is one of the rare references to the revival of an African cultural aesthetic in *Gods of Our Time*, is given full emphasis in Mda's *Ways of Dying*.

# Resistant Form in *Gods of Our Time*

As mentioned, Michael Green identifies two philosophical ideas of history. At the one extreme, there is the refusal to separate history from the present whereby the distinction between past and present collapses (Green, 1997: 22-4). As Raymond Williams points out:

> ...it is necessary to distinguish an important sense of history which is more than, although it includes, organized knowledge of the past.... One way of expressing this new sense is to say that past events are seen not as specific histories but as continuous and connected process. Various systematizations and interpretations of this continuous and connected process then become history in a new general and eventually abstract sense. Moreover...history in many of these uses loses its exclusive association with the past and becomes connected not only to the present but also to the future (quoted in Green, 1997: 22).

Obviously there is the inherent pitfall in this entry to history that the past is domesticated to the present in the sense that the past becomes nothing more than an issue in the politics of the present. Revisionists, for example, may reconstruct the past to authorise their present agendas. As explained by Michel Foucault, continuous history grants the historian a role of controlling the past "without placing him or herself in question" (quoted in Green, 1997: 28). This is for instance the light in which Michael Green sees the social history movement. In form and content the works of social historians are aligned with the literary mode of realism. And, says Green, the author does not question his or her position that the realism of their works masquerades as "a guarantee of the "reality" of their findings", whereby they arrogate to themselves a privileged grasp of reality and the authority of truth (Green, 1997: 27).

To counter this tendency Foucault presents the other mode of historical perception by promulgating a view of the past as an *other* to the present (Green, 1997: 28). According to Poster, he:

> ...attempts to show how the past was different, strange, threatening. He labours to distance the past from the present, to disrupt the easy, cosy intimacy that historians have traditionally enjoyed in the relationship of the past to the present" (quoted in Green, 1997: 28-9).

From this angle the past is allowed to serve as a point of reference that may challenge or pass judgement on the present, which is also an essential quality in Michael Green's theoretical and aesthetic model of "resistant form". But Green adds the caution against Foucault's idea that the past, in foregrounding its difference and alienness, is not estranged from a present perspective, as, say, a romantic mystification of the past would be. A pertinent link must be maintained between the past and the present (Green, 1997: 29, 33).

"Resistant form" may thus be seen as a consensus of the two opposing conceptualisations of history. It entails a use of history that is, at the same time and paradoxically, "...resistant to being simply appropriated by the present and yet relevant enough to relate meaningfully to the present..." (29), or, an approach that "...will make of its own historical material a moment of resistance that leads to an intervention with its own moment of production or consumption" (297).

Obviously, this form of representing history is particularly compelling in a South African context where history has always been a ground of intense contest. Not only has history been manipulated and falsified to justify white hegemony, it may continue to be distorted by such inequalities of representation as exist in the academic production of history. Furthermore, the new political elite is not exempt from exploiting the representation of the past to suit another self-justifying "national" script, at the expense of the histories of the marginalised. A taste of this was experienced when the Truth Commission was about to release its final report in 1998. To most people's surprise, the ANC sought to halt its publication as the report's distinction between a just war and unjust means was regarded as an aim to "criminalize the struggle" (Krog, 1999: 429-35). If the report had been changed to suit the ANC's censored version, it would not only have silenced compelling events in South African history, it would also have denied the victims of ANC violations the recognition of their victimhood. The attempt to stop the report was only prevented because the High Court ruled out the ANC interdict (432-3).

It will be argued here that in spite of the alliance of Wally Serote's novel with the revisionist project of the social historians, in the assertion of people's agency, Serote in *Gods of Our Time* manages not to appropriate his historical material to the present. The resistance movement is foregrounded as the prime mover in the collapse of apartheid, yet it is done in a way that passes judgement on the present rather than endorsing the current structures of power. This has already been shown in Serote's acknowledgement of the complexity of the past, involving both a white conscience and support in the fight of its own regime as well as a revisit with the inevitable instances of betrayal and the crimes committed by the forces of the struggle.

Guha calls attention to the fact that ideological or political predisposition increases the historian's tendency to appropriate the subject of his or her study to serve the purpose of that particular predisposition. "A historiography devoted to [the pursuit of an Ideal Consciousness] (even when that is done, regrettably, in the name of Marxism) is ill-equipped to cope with contradictions which are indeed the stuff history is made of…. Blinded by the glare of a perfect and immaculate Consciousness the [idealising] historian sees nothing, for instance, but solidarity in rebel behaviour and fails to notice its Other, namely, betrayal" (Guha, 1983: 39, 40).

The multi-polar nuances of Serote's representation of the past and the inconsistency he acknowledges at the expense of forged harmony within the resistance movement become no less important when considering Serote's own position at the time of writing the novel as a top member of the ANC, Head of the Department of Arts and Culture and Member of Parliament.

Yet, there are other, related resistant forms in the novel. Firstly, Serote establishes a Foucaultian sense of difference between past and present. Discontinuity between then and now is suggested literally in the temporal setting that stops just short of completing the historical line of continuation that leads to the absolution of the struggle with Mandela's release in 1990 and the subsequent elections in 1994. Instead the narration ends at a point of historical indecisiveness while the resistance against Botha's draconian regime continues. More importantly, this sense of a chunk of time cut off and interrogated independently from the present is enhanced by Serote's forthright refusal to represent the freedom fighters of the past with the hindsight of present knowledge of their eventual victory against the system. This is done, as has been illustrated, by avoiding a simple glorification of the "gods" who fought and sacrificed. Added to the scepticism, doubt, cowardice and times of selfishness in this connection, is an equally honest sense of uncertainty among the activists of where all their efforts will lead to. The characters find it difficult to grasp the ephemeral abstraction of ideals like "freedom" which they have never experienced themselves. One of many examples of this is when Sipho's mother decides to fight:

> She must fight. She had resolved she must fight – how, she did not know, but she must fight, fight for what? For freedom; what is that? (Serote, 1999: 13).

She attempts a provisional answer in blindly contributing to "that which those in prison on Robben Island fight for" (13). The answer of following the leaders and the rhetoric of ideology, more or less blindly, is of no consolation to Lindi, however. Bewildered in a conversation with Moses, she asks: "We are fighting for power?" To which Moses' answer is "Yes". And she continues:

'So we can control?' 'Yes'. 'Control who?' 'Control the wealth of our country so that there is no oppressed or oppressor, white or black, but people building a country which is livable'. 'How do you know that is going to happen?' 'We have the ANC'. 'Why would the ANC not do what the Boers are doing?' (100).

In this way the present South Africa is judged by implying questions such as: have the ideals which these people fought for and died for been achieved? Do we now have an answer to Nomwula's question of what the often used, yet still obscure, word "freedom" is? Is the ANC keeping its promises of alleviating oppression and not instituting a new form of the same thing? In the words of Njabulo Ndebele:

> ...we have to cry out when the past is being deliberately forgotten to ensure that what was gained by it cannot be enjoyed without compunction. It is crucial at this point that the past be seen as a legitimate point of departure for talking about the challenges of the present and the future. The past, no matter how horrible it has been, can redeem us. It can be the moral foundation on which to build the pillars of the future (155).

Even though the past is allowed to stand on its own, severed from the line of causes and effects that lead to the present, without the knowledge of the present state poured into the characters, the psychological pain represented in *Gods of Our Time* is of greater interest to the present, too, than any archaeological curiosity of how life was back then. Indeed the realistic conveyance of the lived experience of pain, suffered by those who sacrificed, institutes an ever present and heavy responsibility on the morrow. First of all there is the responsibility of facilitating the beliefs for which these people fought. Secondly, but equally important, there is the responsibility of never regressing to a situation that would allow a repetition of that kind of suffering. A third point, which will be discussed in more detail in the analysis of *Ways of Dying*, is the implied thread that is drawn in the novel's psychological depiction between the strain imposed on people by history and the current problems of violence.

In relation to the general framework of history writing in South Africa, Serote's novel does resist, in this way, any supremacist script of the past, be it the problems of unequal representation in academic history writing or attempts to obliterate past wrongs in claims of a moral high ground. In that way, *Gods of Our Time* contributes to the democratisation of the country's histories.

However, in terms of the formal relationship between history and literature, there are other considerations to be made about realist novels like Serote's. In regard to the tradition among the oppressed groups in South Africa of recording their revised versions of history in the various genres of arts and literature, J. M. Coetzee argues:

> ...in times of intense ideological pressure like the present, when the space in which the novel and history normally coexist like two cows on the pasture, each minding it own business, is squeezed to almost nothing, the novel, it seems to me, has only two options: supplementarity or rivalry (Attwell, 1990: 101).

Supplementarity was further foregrounded by the social historians when they allotted literature an important function in their project with the argument that literature could enrich history in its capacity of embodying "...the ways of life, patterns of experience, and structures of thought and feeling of communities and classes at large" (Clingman quoted in Green, 1997: 20). The disadvantage of such an intimate relationship with history, seen from a literary point of view, is, as David Attwell points out, that writers, when working within the confines of history are bound to "...play the role of handmaiden to the more powerful, more coherently marshalled, more politically cogent discourses of history" (Green, 1997: 18-9). Accordingly, Serote's novel may be judged, from these criteria, as a mere appendage to the grander narrative of history, "...filling", in the words of Coetzee, "our experience with a certain density of observation" (Attwell, 1990: 101).

In contrast, says Coetzee, fiction written in rivalry to history will free literature from the discourse of history, in an assertion of literary independence. The rival mode:

> ...operates in terms of its own procedures and issues in its own conclusions..., [it] evolves its own paradigms and myths, in the process...perhaps going as far as to show up the mythic status of history – in other words, demythologzing history (quoted in Green, 1997: 21).

As will be shown in the following analysis, this is the theoretical framework within which Mike Nicol operates, thus marking a great contrast in form to Serote's realist camaraderie with history. In content, it should be added, we move from the history of the oppressed to that of the accountable oppressors.

# Mike Nicol: *The Ibis Tapestry*

*The Ibis Tapestry* is structured on the simple plot of a "whodunit" thriller. The dull everyday life of the newly divorced pulp fiction writer, Robert Poley, is abruptly intersected when a laptop computer mysteriously arrives in his mail containing the creative, cryptic and conscience-ridden writings of the recently murdered, illegal arms trader, Christo Mercer. Intrigued by Mercer's troubled psyche and his clandestine enterprise with its links to the apartheid regime, Poley starts to assemble the social, political, personal and fictional unveilings, leading up to the crucial questions of who killed Mercer and why – the answers to which will no doubt shed some light on the corrupt and ruthless pattern of the old order. The cues Poley has to go on combine historical information and interviews with Mercer's relatives and associates, but the first lead is Mercer's personal obsession with Christopher Marlowe's play of Machiavellian power, *Tambourlaine the Great*. Mercer's rewriting of this Elizabethan play appears to stand as his key confessional. Particularly his revisit with the central part of the play, the atrocious killing of four virgins outside the town walls of besieged Damascus, is revealing in that respect, as it is used allegorically by Mercer to recapitulate the uncannily similar incident when his client, the warlord Ibn el-Tamaru, repeats the act of the play by gunning down four virgins in a remote Saharan town called Djano. The only difference between the event in the play and the one in North Africa is that a victim, Salma, survives in the latter to tell the story of the violation.

Although *The Ibis Tapestry* is set in contemporary South Africa and its focus is on the act of the present resuscitation of the past, the work may still be regarded as a historical novel. As Michael Green demonstrates, the academic perception of history has undergone some tremendous changes in the latter half of the twentieth century. Among these changes, the distinction in the traditional view of history between past and present has collapsed with the modern truism that history is largely a product of the present (21-4). Green quotes R. G. Collingwood:

> ...since the past in itself is nothing, the knowledge of the past is not, and cannot be, the historian's goal. His goal...is knowledge of the present; to that everything must return, round that everything must revolve. But, as historian, he is concerned with one special aspect of the present – how it came to be what it is. In this sense, the past is an aspect or function of the present...(223).

Another way of putting this is that the perception of a connectedness between the present and the past in a unified sense of history, places the present in the realm of history just as much as the past (Green: 21-4). Correspondingly, the classical definition of the historical novel, to which *Gods of Our Time* conforms, as a category of novels contending exclusively with past events, is extended to include novels of the present. A novel like *The Ibis Tapestry* is concerned, to emphasise Collingwood's phrasing, "with that special aspect of the present – how it came to be".

Evidently, the novel's detective story structure perfectly matches Collingwood's postulation. As Green points out, the detective, in this case Poley, is occupied in the present with the circumstances behind a crime that went before the narrative itself. In the words of Green:

> Detective fiction...presents the perfect model for grasping the present as history as its temporal implications are the inverse of the conventional historical mode: it is focussed on the present but governed by an event in the (recent) past (224).

The detective element of *The Ibis Tapestry* may be read as an analogy of the Truth and Reconciliation Commission, a reading that is further supported by the similarities between Poley's difficulties of recovering a picture of the past from confessions and witness testimonies and the experience of the Truth Commission. Certainly *The Ibis Tapestry* concerns itself with one of the central problems of the Truth Commission, the fact that only the tip of the iceberg was disclosed, as findings produced even more questions than answers because of withheld information and the refusal to participate by key figures and institutions. With the Truth Commission at the back of the mind, the following analysis will look at two of the main themes that run through Nicol's novel: guilt and remembering.

As said, Christo Mercer's conscience is troubled by his client, Ibn el-Tamaru's gunning down of four virgins outside the town walls of Djano. In addition to that, there are indicia that he, as a young recruit in the South African army, participated in massacres in Angola of innocent civilians and, finally, there are traces, although prohibitively shadowy, that Mercer was involved in state-sponsored training of Inkatha cadres to empower these in the war against the UDF – the apartheid equivalent of the colonial divide and rule strategy.

However, a great amount of uncertainty surrounds these flashes of Mercer's hidden past. The lack of clarity can be ascribed mainly to the fact that the investigative process is hampered by a scarcity of documents and obscured by cardinal informants. Mercer's confession, for instance, remains enigmatic and shrouded by the fact that Ibn el-Tamaru's cruel story foregrounds his own. Likewise, the interviews Poley conducts with people who were close to Mercer are muddled by defensive objectives of withholding crucial information and relating only biased versions of the story. As with the Truth Commission, most of the key individuals refuse to speak at all (114-33 and 152-8).

Although Poley succeeds in establishing a fairly unequivocal picture of Mercer's responsibility in gunrunning and war crimes, he admits, at the end, that he has failed to fulfil the initial aim of answering the questions of *who* killed Christo Mercer and *why*. Undoubtedly, these answers would have led to a disclosure of a far greater network of perpetration, possibly involving Third Force activities with links right to the top of the apartheid state. As it is, only a partial light has been shed on the gloomy past. In that way Poley's conclusion echoes the evaluation of the truth Commission after the release of its final report in 1998. Summing up Antjie Krog states that the Commission "succeeded fairly well in establishing the factual truth, in determining 'what happened'", while it was "far less successful in convincing South Africans of the moral truth, 'who was responsible'" (448). This can be ascribed to the fact that it was only the small lackeys, the "Christo Mercers", who testified. As in *The Ibis Tapestry*, the top end of the line of command contributed with no or very little information. P.W. Botha, the mastermind behind the destabilisation wars in Southern Africa and the Third Force activities (see Krog, 1994: 310-11, 90-104), refused to appear before the commission at all (Krog, 1999: 401-11); his successor, De Klerk, made only a brief, dispassionate and defensive statement, denying any knowledge of Third Force perpetrations and the state-instigated violence in Kwa-Zulu Natal while in office (189-95). Likewise the South African Defence Force revealed nothing, nor did the Commission want to jeopardise the fragile peace between the ANC and Inkatha by summoning Inkatha's leader, Mangosuthu Buthelezi (Weekly Mail & Guardian, 1998: 2). Finally, the leadership of the ANC were granted amnesties without any public hearings and Winnie Mandela denied all allegations of human rights violations directed at her and her gang of thugs, the Mandela Football Club (Krog, 1999: 387-89).

In the face of such great gaps in the location of responsibility, literature may prove to be an enabling medium that can break the silences caused in the historical discourse by its foundation on the documentation of evidence. *The Ibis Tapestry* may be interpreted in this light, and in contrast to Serote's novel which stays within the conventions of historical discourse, Nicol seeks to redefine the conditions of value between history and literature. By deconstructing the discourse of history, he seeks not to reduce the value of history, but to expand the scope and value of fiction, in concord with Coetzee's rival mode, as an independent channel of a truer truth of the past.

First of all, Nicol questions the authenticity of the methodology in historical writing.

In contrast to the narrative voice in Serote's novel, in accord with the narrative voice in historiography, whose reliability is never questioned, the narrative in *The Ibis Tapestry* is of a most uncertain nature. Apart from the bias in the interviews and the indeterminate nature of Mercer's written confession, even Poley's voice, which is our prime channel to the story, is to be regarded with suspicion. He is self-consciously aware of his story as a subjective construction: "I am the writer.... I choose what to include and what to leave out" (81). This stance becomes particularly dubious as concerns the factual truth value of his presentation of the story, when his mother informs the reader that Poley is unreliable with an inclination to exaggerate and blow everything out of proportion (81). In this way Nicol joins the line of writers and critics who revolt against the implied assumption in realist writing and history projects that historical narrative is capable of neutrality and that written and oral sources provide an unmediated access to the reality or "lived experience" of the past. In regard of the testimonies and confessions in the Truth and Reconciliation Commission, Nicol corroborates Antjie Krog's observation that:

> [i]n every story there is a hearsay, there is grouping together, there are assumptions, there are exaggerations to bring home the enormities of situations, there is downplaying to confirm innocence. And all of this together makes up the whole country's truth, so also the lies. And the stories that date from earlier times (259).

The slippery nature of narrative disrupts the standard notions of objectivity and certainty, which have traditionally lent authority to the narrative of history and which are likewise presupposed in the claim to the "authenticity" of the oral testimony that informs the project of the Truth Commission (Minkley and Rassool, 1998: 91). Or, to put it another way, history's privilege of being perceived as having a direct relationship with reality and thus having an exclusive claim to represent reality "empirically" or "as it really was" is rejected. Instead history has come to be seen as no more than a discourse, and, like any other discourse, subject to the ever partisan medium of language, which, in the words of Bakhtin, is "overpopulated with the intentions of others" (quoted in Hutcheon, 1988: 80).

The erosion of authority and objectivity in the narrative voice in *The Ibis Tapestry* is accompanied by a correlated postmodern assault on history through the annotation that the past is only available to us in a textual form. Just as history, whether in the form of oral testimony or writing, cannot produce an objective or transparent account of any certain actuality, so the textuality of our knowledge of the past is inescapable: "the past arrives in the forms of texts and textual remainders – memories, reports, published writings, archives, monuments, and so forth", leaving it impossible to know past in its entirety (Dominick LaCapra quoted in Hutcheon, 1988: 129). There are several expressions of this stance in Nicol's novel. For one thing the mentioned self-awareness of the author prevents the text from creating any conventional narrative illusion. The same effect is obtained by the intersections of critical notes and references to other works that interrupt the rare occasions when the writer absents himself. As a result the reader's attention always returns to the act of writing itself, leaving no room for imagining that the narration is more than a textual construction.

The use of many layers of intertextuality is another way in which Nicol emphasises the textual nature of history. Like two opposite mirrors, the narrative of the novel is a reflection of texts within texts within texts. Nicol tells the story of Poley who tells the story of Mercer whose confession is structured on the story of the surviving victim Salma, and so on. Likewise, Christopher Marlowe's play of ruthless violence and oppression *Tambourlaine the Great* runs as a parallel text to both Christo Mercer's life, Ibn el-Tamaru's, and as an overall allegory of the apartheid state. Meanwhile, the most apparent advocacy of the world, or history, as text is the creation myth which el-Tamaru's wife passes on to Salma:

> In my country we believed the ibis hatched the world and *named* it. She made *letters* from the slopes of mountains, the contortions of trees, the sloughed skins of snakes, from the tracks of beetles left over sand. She made *words* from the sounds of the wind. These she sprinkled about the earth as she flew and they *named* places where they fell.... She had the magic of *words* and *writing* (italics added) (61).

The "hatching" of the world in its signified form is granted less space than a sentence in this myth and is completely overshadowed by the creation of signifiers (names, letters, words and writing). Accordingly the importance of the ibis' creation seems to rest with the world as text, since herein lie the codes of man as a social being: our ability to communicate, to render the world and pass on our experiences to each other and future generations will always be restricted to the textuality of signs and language.

When history has been deconstructed, in this way, or "demythologized" as Coetzee has it, from an uninhibited medium of the "real" world to a form that recreates the world as subjective text, or, as Hayden White says, to a form that is discursively affiliated with the narrative of literature, history levels with and may freely interact with other forms of text (White, 1987: 44). Accordingly, when metaphor or metonymy is lacking in one discourse, like the history of apartheid atrocity, it may be retrieved from another, such as an Elizabethan play. As Linda Hutcheon says:

> The authority of any act of writing is put into question by locating the discourses of both history and fiction within an ever-expanding intertextual network that mocks any notion of either single origin or simple causality (1988: 129).

One outgrowth of the free interaction of texts is that texts begin to repeat and imitate themselves. According to Michel Foucault:

The frontiers of a book are never clear-cut: beyond the title, the first lines, and the last full-stop, beyond its internal configuration and its autonomous form, it is caught up in a system of references to other books, other texts, other sentences: it is a node within a network (quoted in Hutcheon, 1988: 127).

The textual repetitions inevitably end in parody as "the intertexts of history and fiction take on parallel status in the parodic reworking of the textual past of both the 'world and literature'" (Hutcheon, 1988: 124)[9], and in the act corrupting "...the notion of the original as rare, single, and valuable" (Hutcheon; 1989: 94).

The examples of parodied repetition of literature and history in *The Ibis Tapestry* are numerous. Christopher Marlowe is impersonated in, and lexically linked with, Christo Mercer. Each is the creator of a tale of political monsters (who are equally cloned by initial letters): Marlowe creates Tambourlaine and Mercer creates Tamaru. The only difference is that Marlowe "trades in software" whereas Mercer trades in "hardware" (141). Similarly, the shooting down of the four virgins is repeated over and over again. It is first recorded in Marlowe's play, then in Ibn el-Tamaru's attack on Djano and thirdly in Mercer's dreams and confession. One tragicomic example of a parodied revisit with history that needs mention, because it exemplifies the theme and its implications so well, is the case of the diet in the English concentration camps during the Anglo-Boer War (1899-1902). It has been claimed that Afrikaner women and children who were interned in the camps were fed on a diet containing crushed glass which supposedly caused the widespread affliction of dysentery that mostly ended in agonising death. As the narrator ruminates, this piece of history finds its grotesque repetition on the shelves of supermarkets today, in the form of a laxative which, containing magnesium sulphate that resembles ground glass, is commonly known as "Engelse Sout" (Afrikaans: "English Salt") (135).

The postmodernist fluidity between discourses of fiction and history and the refusal to accept any possibility of transparent representation of reality has aroused strong reactions from various sides. Diana Brydon, for instance, summarises many arguments when she states that postmodernism, at its worst, implies a denial that things happened at all. At its best, she continues, postmodernism may not deny the past, but the focus on "history's textualised accessibility" and "problems of representation" involves an "impossibility of retrieving truth" (Brydon, 1995:142). This in turn, adds Kwame Appiah, prevents any concern for the human suffering for the victimised (Appiah, 1995:123). The concern behind this line of argument came to the fore in some of the reactions to Antjie Krog's documentary work on the Truth and Reconciliation Commission, *Country of My Skull* in which Krog insists on the value of "different versions" and perspectives of the past as well as the notion of "plural truths" (Krog, 1999: 299-300). This provoked Claudia Braude to equate Krog's platform with the denials of the National Party: "She takes liberties of creativity in the question of ethics" echoing "...the NP's warning to the TRC of "the elusive nature of truth" and reminding of De Klerk's submission to the Truth Commission which stated that "[p]erceptions of what is true vary from time to time, from place to place and from party to party". At the end of the day, argues Braude, *Country of My Skull* "...helps decriminalising the NP" (9).

Although Krog's work differs from Nicol's, the concern of the sceptics remains the same. The postmodernist shelling of history as indeterminate as well as its perception of truth and the representation of reality as textual and subjective entails an ambivalence towards history, which, at its worst, may be exploited for purposes of de-emphasising or even a denying the injustice committed by the apartheid regime and the inexplicable pain inflicted on the people who were excluded.

It may be argued, however, that such alarm is generated by a misconception of postmodernist strategies. Certainly Mike Nicol's novel provides no basis for historical denial, nor even, in message, the slightest minimization of the cruelty of South Africa's past. In fact, as it will be shown, the uncertainty of the narrative voice and the parodic intertextualisation of history and fiction are employed to counter exactly this.

Linda Hutcheon brings the relation between postmodernism and the past back on track:

> To speak of provisionality and indeterminacy is not to deny historical knowledge...what the postmodern writing of both history and literature has taught us is that both history and fiction are discourses, that both constitute systems of signification by which we make sense of the past.... In other words, the meaning and shape are not *in the 'events'*, but *in the systems* which make those past 'events' into present historical 'facts'. This is not a 'dishonest refuge from truth' but an acknowledgement of the meaning-making function of human constructs (1988: 88-9).

When applying this theory, the weight of the problem in *The Ibis Tapestry* shifts away from the great uncertainties of what *exactly* happened in the past to *how* that past, be it factually concrete or elusive, may be processed in the present or passed on to the future. In other words, what "systems of meaning-making", what discourses, may enjoy that privilege? The answer to the question is obvious. On account of Nicol's intertextual use of history and literature, no discourse should prevail over another. The "master-narrative" of history that previously enjoyed a status as *the* foremost discourse in which the past should be preserved, has been demystified, in a Coetzeean sense, to a level of equality with all other texts.

The potential gains from such a democratisation of the uses of history are manifold. Narratives across different forms of discourse may enrich each other. The intertextualisation of history and fiction, or the narrativisation of history, enables Nicol to create a moral universe that subordinates such problems in historiography as lacking evidence, as in the example of the silences in historical projects when it comes to the location of the apartheid leadership's responsibility for commanding human rights violations.

With a seeming reference to the evanescent character of the truth in TRC testimonies and confessions as well as the heap of contradicting or missing information, Poley muses: "In a true story accuracy is the first victim" (147). With one stroke, and in a Ndebelean thrust of transforming reader consciousness, all the problems pertaining to exaggerations and extenuations of narrative are swept aside as insignificant. Factual accuracy is not the only passage to truth. In fact, our preoccupation with factual accuracy often obscures the clarity of what is true. As Poley's literary mentor, Professor Khufalo states in an elaboration on Poley's idea: "The essence of truth lies not in facts, Robert, but in form. We're convinced not by what is said, but how it's said" – hence the attention drawn by Hutcheon from *events* to the *meaning-making systems* – "And sometimes, to arrive at a greater truth – something more truthful than what happened, our language forces us to, how shall I put it...invent?" (147). This parallels the gist of the argument behind Coetzee's advocacy of a literature in rivalry with the supremacy of the historical discourse in questions of what is true and false:

> ...history is not reality; […] history is a kind of discourse; […] the novel is a kind of discourse; […] inevitably, in our culture, history will, with varying degrees of forcefulness, try to claim primacy, claim to be a master-form of discourse, just as, inevitably, people like myself will defend themselves by saying that history is nothing but a certain kind of story that people have agreed to tell each other.... [Wherefore] the categories of history are not privileged. They do not reside in reality: they are a certain construction upon reality (Attwell, 1990: 102-3).

Whereas the historical discourse of the Truth and Reconciliation Commission suffers from gaps in the location of responsibility, represented in Poley's failure to determine who killed Mercer and why, the form of *The Ibis Tapestry* places an inescapable guilt on the apartheid regime and its cohorts. Although Mercer's co-directors in Precision Engineering echo the apartheid leaders at TRC hearings in their denial of the illegal arms trade, they are unable to parry the "kkk" that flickers from their names, Kirkland and Kleinsmith (152-3). Similarly Frederick de Klerk's denial of having any knowledge of the Third Force as well as his euphemistic veil of apartheid as merely "a system that didn't work" (quoted in Brink, 1991: 3) are invalidated not only by the satire of the corresponding three "k"s in his name but also by the allegory of Marlowe's play. Like the "Mercers", De Klerk is an integrated part of the overall story of "rampant titanism" that has infected this world since times immemorial. The leadership of apartheid who evaded judgement in the TRC hearings, due to their politically privileged positions, do not escape judgement in literature. And, to repeat Coetzee's rival form, the novel succeeds in operating "in terms of its own procedures and issues its own conclusions" in the sense that the technical understanding of guilt in the discourse of history is undertoned and amplified instead as a much more complex matter in literature.

In Nicol's novel, the ibis is the absolute judge. After it had named the world, the creation myth continues:

> She had no other words for what happened in these places between these animals. She had to wait until the events occurred. She had to leave the story to us. "Who you are", she warned our ancestors, "will be known by the tales you tell. These I cannot alter. But I shall judge you by them both in this world and the next" (61).

Consequently, De Klerk, "Mercer", and anyone who took part in the story of oppression in South Africa will be judged forever in our stories. The ibis stalked like sentinels outside the town walls of Damascus, outside Djano, in Angola (19, 157) and, "after the event", it was pictured in a bead tapestry, as in words, by the violated Salma: the judgement is woven by our stories into the tapestry of our collective lives, countering the silences, euphemisms and evasions of de Klerk and other leaders. Or to contextualise this with Jackson's theories, the political deals at the top of society which allowed people like De Klerk and P. W. Botha to stay in control of part of the nation's history are countered in literature, and the authority of the story is reclaimed. Here, the true verdict of history occurs when history passes into literary myth and metaphor, like Nicol's deliberations on the "Engelse Sout" on the shelves in South African supermarkets.

In inseparable congruence with the cultural sentence of the guilty, one of the main concerns in Nicol's novel is to deter forgetting. Another, equally important, effect of the narrative uncertainty and intertextuality, in that respect, is that their inconclusive nature opens up the text and discourages the formation of a closure to history. There is an ambition in traditional history writing to resolve the past by providing answers to "how", "why", and "when" armoured with the "scientific" methodologies of teleology and causality. This tends not only to fix history within an apparently totalising system of coherent unified meaning (Hutcheon, 1989: 62-70), it also implies the sense of a crevice between the past and the present where the wrongs of the past are isolated in time as bygones in the light of a new rectified present. In sharp contrast, the uncertainty of narrative in Nicol's novel refuses any resolution of the past by leaving the crucial questions unanswered. As a result, the "not knowing" continues to haunt the present, preventing the comfort of leaving its cruelty behind as history. As Timothy Jones observes, *The Ibis Tapestry* collides with our hunger for the kind of omniscient knowledge of the past which "will put a stop to time" (141). Instead, the past will forever be a haunting factor in the present, resisting its passive conservation in dusty history books and everyday disregard. Its very unresolvedness will keep feeding our imagination and creativity with stories that may eventually transmute into a cultural memory and awareness of guilt and responsibility.

Likewise history's taming and mastery of the past, coated in the pretence of scientific objectivity, may prevent the extension of the boundaries of the thinkable. Whereas apartheid in historical discourse is singularised as an event, within a limited range of explanation such as group politics and capitalist control of the work force,

Nicol's intertextualisation of the country's past with literary history opens the possibilities of interpretation on a far greater scale. The forces that created the times of torturing, murdering and spying in Elizabethan England are no different from those of apartheid South Africa. They are the forces of rampant power that have been allowed to breed and terrorise the world since times immemorial. Where historical methodology of cause and effect puts an end to every event in history, be it the First World War, the Holocaust, the genocide in Rwanda or apartheid, history in Nicol is linked up in a ceaseless repetition of the same story, despite the fact that human kind has had aeons of experience. The moral predilection that Nicol openly intermixes with history may lead the thoughts onto Liisa Malkki's cautions against the tendency to turn historical events into instruments of moral politics. However, although Nicol does amalgamate history and morals, he does so not in favour of one political faction against another, he does so with an appeal to all human kind to recognise a universal burden of guilt brought down on us from our collective past.

Repetition of history can only be blamed on our failure to develop a higher form of humanity, which is encoded in the mutually enforcing fallacies of forgetting and divorcing past wrongs from a supposedly different present. In the words of Milan Kundera, "the struggle of man against power", and hence the struggle of man against the repetition of history, "is the struggle of memory against forgetting" (quoted in Cohen, 1994: xiii). Accordingly it is the display in literature of history's repetition of itself as well as the recognition of history as a place of ache and discomfort, as Frederic Jameson puts it, that ensure remembering (quoted in Green, 1997: 268). Says Ndebele, it is literature of such transformative power that "contribute[s] to bringing about a highly conscious, sensitive new person in a new society" (1994: 73).

There is, however, one significant divergence in *The Ibis Tapestry* that breaks the spell of historical repetition. In contrast to the plot in Christopher Marlowe's play, and in contrast to the records of history writ large, the victim, Salma, survives and, more importantly, is allowed and even promoted to voice her version of the story. Salma's testimony is given both as the tapestry of beads that pictures the judging ibis and in Mercer's recounting of Ibn el-Tamaru's perpetration in which Salma is the first-person narrator. She makes an obvious parallel to the victims' hearings in the Truth Commission which have been regarded by many observers as a diversion, like Salma, from the customary course of history and thus widely acclaimed as the Commission's greatest achievement. Antjie Krog remarks:

> If the TRC is regarded as an effort to create a forum for victims to bring some form of balance to the political amnesty, then the Commission succeeded in a most remarkable way. The experiences of victims did indeed become part of the national psyche and part of our country's acknowledged history for the first time (448-49).

In Jackson's terminology, the TRC is an institution that provides public recognition of the stories of the oppressed. Through this recognition, the perpetrated may gain a sense of control over the perpetrators and a sense of re-established influence on the world as their stories may come to play a role in changing the collective memory and identity. as Jackson puts it, individual stories are de-individualised in the process of becoming fit for public appearance and by that they flow into the collective ethos (Jacskon, 2002: 26).

Salma's very presence has consequences at several levels, alternating the otherwise habitual path of privilege for the perpetrating party. For one thing, she poses a threat to those who have something to hide, which is indicated in the suggestions of Mercer becoming increasingly agitated after the idea of a truth commission was first mentioned in 1994 (130-1). Moreover, as Professor Khufalo states, it would have devastated Tambourlaine's wife, Zenocrate, had there been a surviving victim in Marlowe's play, as Zenocrate was furnished with all the conscience that Tambourlaine was completely devoid of. As it is, there was no survivor in the play and Zenocrate was accordingly acquitted with intense but survivable pangs of conscience. In *The Ibis Tapestry*, Salma's survival drives Sarra, el-Tamaru's wife and Zenocrate's equivalent, to commit suicide. She considers herself as responsible as her husband in causing Salma's misery (with an obvious reference to the guilt of all South Africans who either granted the National Party their support in elections or indirectly by remaining passive). Consequently, she becomes obsessed with paying penance and atoning for Salma's suffering, and unlike Zenocrate who regards it as her forced and cursed fate to follow Tambourlaine (Marlowe, 1902: Act 1, sc. II and Act 3, sc. II), Sarra's emotional tie with the victim causes her, sub-/consciously, to defy Ibn el-Tamaru and his desires for her. She manages more or less to reconcile with Salma in opposition to oppressive power, but never to overcome the burden of guilt.

Although Ibn el-Tamaru carries on his evil mission remorselessly, the survival of the victim also has repercussions for him. He never overcomes the infliction of grief that hits him at Sarra's death and, Salma, whom he blames for poisoning his wife with guilt and hence for driving her away from him and life, has deprived him of his villainous offspring.

Guilt, if absent in el-Tamaru, is forcefully present in Christo Mercer. In fact, what seems to have inspired Mercer to draw the analogy between el-Tamaru and Sarra, or Tambourlaine and Zenocrate, and his own life in the first place appears to be the division of character between the completely debauched and the completely remorseful. But in contrast with el-Tamaru and Sarra, Mercer embodies both. The exact point at which he discovered the presence of this duality within himself was in Angola, when he killed the Cuban soldier, Jorge Morate. Although Morate is shot, he lives on to terrorise Mercer's Zenocratic conscience, notably in the many nightmares that start at that time and persist until his death. The "poisoning", the injection of guilt, is symbolised in the foul smell of onions that Morate exhales as he departs, which replaces Mercer's taste for onion since the innocent days of childhood with a haunting, almost psychotic, avoidance of it (128-9 and 172-3).

Although his burden of guilt does not effect any gesture of contrition towards the hurt, like Sarra devoting her entire life to Salma, Mercer's awareness of right and wrong, prompted by the presence of victims, causes the self-inflicted penance of a tormented conscience that links him with the character of Sarra. In fact the two theories Poley raises about the causes of Mercer's death both involve a symbolic connection between Mercer and Sarra: either he provoked his own murder in a suicidal confrontation with a gang of thugs or he was silenced by his own network of criminals as they began to lose faith in his loyalty. Whichever theory is correct, Mercer's Zenocratic conscience imbues him with a compulsion, in the words of Khufalo, "to be the first to testify in a truth commission", wherefore the Zenocratic conscience is strong enough to drive him to suicide or his collaborators to take a considerable interest in silencing him. The form, the intertextual connection, then, once again, presents a truth that ranges beyond the uncertainty of fact.

The survival of victims and their ability to speak thus represents the greatest compulsion for the guilty and is one of the strongest bulwarks against repeating history in the future. It is the weight of the victims' presence, through testimonies like Salma's, that either isolates destructive forces, like Sarra isolating el-Tamaru and denying him the conception that would allow him and his kind any posterity, or leads to a self-destructive self-interrogation as in the case of Mercer. Moreover, the fact that the victims' hearings of the Truth Commission have become part of the "national psyche" and "acknowledged history", as Krog claims, may engender the preventive impact of a lasting national memory of pain and shame. Ultimately, in the words of Krog:

> If [the TRC] sees truth as the widest possible compilation of people's perceptions, stories, myths and experiences, it will have chosen to restore memory and foster a new humanity, and perhaps that is justice in its deepest sense (23).

However, Nicol is well aware that the repentance of Mercer and Sarra are somewhat utopian idealisations. Reality hosts more people without scruples like Ibn el-Tamaru, or people who would rather preach unawareness or innocence than lose face. Hence victims' accounts are not enough. With the Truth Commission it soon became clear that the possibility of reconciliation rested with victims' willingness to forgive rather than perpetrators' display of remorse. Although many white South Africans do feel remorse (see Antjie Krog, 1999: 223 and 436), Antjie Krog illustrates the indifference of the privileged in South Africa who have no sense of collective guilt whatsoever and are "ensconced in so much financial and political fortune" that nothing in their lives has changed (Krog, 1998: 404). One of the many incidents that make this clear was at a hearing in the Northern Province: "While the Commission listens to testimony of human rights violations, cheerful white families with their Tupperware, their sunhats and their small-town familiarity spend the day picnicking on the grass outside" (296-7). Inasmuch as Nicol thus endorses the principles of the TRC of the opportunity for victims to write history and, ideally, the opportunity for perpetrators to show remorse and hence make a step towards reconciliation, *The Ibis Tapestry* contains a radical stance against the appeal to forgiveness. This bearing should also be seen in the light of resisting any closure to history.

When Poley interviews Salma, her view counters many of the astonishing stories from the Truth Commission of victims who readily forgive unmentionable crimes:

> If I forgave I would not be freed. I would still have the pain. I would not be healed. I would still be ashamed that I had been allowed to live. It would be too easy to forgive him, too easy. So my choice was to accuse him. To judge him. Like the ibis I had to judge him...for those who were dead. But not only for them, also for those who had chosen to forget (198).

What is suggested in Salma's view is that forgiveness easily frees the perpetrators from their guilt and in that way cancels the past. As pointed out by Anthony Holiday:

> ...forgiving is a species of forgetting which severs the remorseful tie fettering authors of evil to those they have harmed, so that the latter no longer haunt the former. When we say to someone who expresses remorse for a wrong they have done us, 'Let's forget it,' it is a release of this order we afford them. We are offering an absolution – which may or may not be conditional on retribution or restitution – such that past evils no longer exert a claim on us or those who have visited evil on us (44).

Forgiveness thus entails a dangerous closure against remembering and presents an opening to communal amnesia on the part of the guilty sections of society – it makes it very easy to shrug off the burden of the past and picnic next to it without any consideration of personal responsibility. Salma sees it as the victim's task to compel remembrance and institute by her presence a perpetual emblem of liability:

> I reminded him of what he was. I do not think there can be any forgiving and there should be no forgetting. Ibn el-Tamaru was a killer and will always be that and so forever he will be unforgiven (198).

The constant reminding prevents the perpetrator from ever being freed of history's burden of guilt. What is moreover involved in this ethical perspective is that the responsibility of reconciliation is rightfully shifted from the victim onto the shoulder of the guilty party. Like Sarra, the guilty are sentenced to a role in humiliation to the wronged with an obligation to accommodate the needs of the victimised in unremitting indebtedness.

In many ways Nicol thus seems to introduce in South Africa, in resistance to the national appeals to forgiveness, the idea which Derek Walcott called the "truly tough aesthetic of the New World" (Walcott, 1995: 371). Walcott, in critical response to "the literature of revenge written by the descendants of slaves" and "the literature of remorse written by the descendants of masters", champions a "truly tough" literature that "neither explains nor forgives history" (371). As has been illustrated, Nicol refuses to explain the history of apartheid with a methodology that, in the words of Walcott "justifies, explains and expiates" (373). Instead history reflects itself in endless textuality that escapes any rationalising closure. There is no resolve and consequently it will continue to haunt our minds. Likewise there is no closure that would make forgetting easy. Redemption is suspended for the guilty and their descendants, just as in the case of the Germans in relation to the Jews. At one point in her coverage of the Truth Commission, Krog asks a Jewish colleague what gestures of contrition were made by Germany after the Holocaust. She is given an astounding list, including more than a hundred billion dollars that turned Israel into an industrialised state. The realisation that not even the slightest hint of forgiveness can be traced in Jewish communities, despite such considerable reparation, overcomes her like a nauseating seizure (197 and 437).

As for the victims, there is no relief of the pain and Salma seems to incarnate Walcott's tough aesthetic insofar as her creative revisions of the past cannot bring any deliverance, only acceptance. It is Sarra who realises this:

> From the servants I heard that you'd brought the ibis. I heard them call you a child of hope. But I know there are wounds which never heal. Unseen, hidden wounds. Sometimes their pain is dimmed, sometimes for years there is no pain at all! But the wounds have not healed: they wait, bloody and raw. Those I cannot heal, though I can help you learn to accept them. In talking about them, describing them, there is a kind of hope (48).

Although Serote does not explicitly engage in the question of forgiveness, due to his portrayal of the oppressed leans more towards active self-assertion than passive victimisation, there is also a hint of the "truly tough aesthetic" in *Gods of Our Time*. First of all, despite the gesture towards reconciliation in his attempt to nuance the previous black / white polarisation, there is an implicit demand in the realist descriptions that the times be remembered for all their sordidness which is, arguably, given further momentum by the disconcerting absence in the novel of any consideration of forgiveness. Likewise the change of consciousness that is proposed in Lindi's song, and in the novel as a whole, does not involve wiping clean the slate of the past. Rather, it has been shown, there is only the promise of an acceptance of the wounds as in Salma's tapestry.

# Resistant Form in *The Ibis Tapestry*

As has been explicated before, Michael Green's resistant form pivots around a differential use of history that may pass recurrent judgement on the present. The idea of judgement is carved out by Frederic Jameson:

> ...the very dynamics of the historical tribunal are unexpectedly and dialectically reversed: it is not we who sit in judgement on the past, but rather the past...which judges us, imposing the painful knowledge of what we are not, what we are no longer, what we are not yet (quoted in Green, 1997: 174).

When literature then treats the present as history, as Nicol does in problematising the contemporary engagement with the past, its resistant form lies within its capability of creating "within the present the necessary difference from which to "judge the present" (Green, 1997: 180). In other words, the resistant form in *The Ibis Tapestry* is to be found in the problematisation of the current ways of recuperating from the past.

The resistant form may therefore be illustrated in the subversion of the formal conventions of the detective genre which shares a number of similarities with the digging up of the past in conventional history writing. As in a "whodunit", the novel sets out to refamiliarise the present with the past, to domesticate the past and, like the Truth Commission and other historical undertakings, to establish as clear a picture as possible of past violations. Accordingly, Poley manages to disclose a fair amount of detail of the life and crimes of Christo Mercer through a methodological approach that is part of the discipline of conventional history writing. Says Foucault:

> [Historians] often assume that their principal aim should be to render [their] subject matter 'familiar' to their readers. What appears strange at first glance must be shown in the course of the narrative to have had sufficient reasons for its occurrence and therefore susceptible to understanding by ordinary informed common sense... By rendering the strange familiar, the historian divests the human world of the mystery in which it comes clothed (Hayden White on Foucault, quoted in Green, 1997: 144).

However, the attempt to conquer the alienness of the past places the present in an unfavourably imperious position in relation to the foregoing, exercising dominance, in the words of Green, by "controlling the past through knowing it" (28).

Yet, the conventions of the detective story, and thus the conventions of historical discourse, erode in *The Ibis Tapestry* as the genre's crucial questions of "who?" and "why?" are never answered. In that way, the history of Third Force perpetration remains shrouded in a great deal of uncertainty. The similarities in this respect between Poley's investigations and the concluding evaluations of the Truth and Reconciliation Commission do not dispirit Nicol, nor does he leave the inescapable uncertainty of historical fact in the hands of forces of denial. Rather, he turns uncertainty into an enabling factor by deploying a literary strategy and a theoretical light which applauds uncertainty; that is, postmodernism. Instead of being a negative vagueness or elusiveness, historical uncertainty then forces history into becoming positively defamiliarised, in antithesis to the historian's "principal aim" as summarised by Foucault. And to recapitulate Foucault's preferred alternative, which was explained in the Serote analysis, Nicol represents the past in its uncertainty as "different, strange, threatening", thus disrupting "the easy, cosy intimacy that historians have traditionally enjoyed in the relationship of the past to the present". Moreover, as a true resistant form in agreement with Green's prescriptions, the distance that is thus created between the past and present is a distance of relevance that places the past in judgement of the present and the future. This is done at two interrelated levels. Firstly, the missing information or the absence of historical certainty represents a haunting unresolvedness of history, compels the cruelty of the past to remain a continual critical and disturbing factor in the contemporaneity. It becomes impossible to "control the past through knowing it" and, in Walcott's terms, history shuns being settled through explanation. Secondly, it is precisely the "not knowing", the sense of unresolved business, that allows for an alternative discourse in Coetzeean rivalry with history. The absence of a solid grasp of the past both demythologises the meaning-making systems of any essentialising historical discourse. Room is opened for other discourses. Literature may exploit this room to seize control of the silences imposed on history by the political elite. The silences may be filled with parody, satire and counter-myths, which as it all seeps into the taxonomy of cultural memory, may turn into a reference-point of judging authority and the forces of forgetting. Again, the myths that may be spun in this context are not the kind that may become instrumental in group politics; they are subversive and anti-authoritarian, keeping a check on the present with the lever of a history of collective wrongs.

Another, inseparable and perhaps more tangible, resistance to the present is the novel's opposition to the current ideological pressure for forgiveness. As has been argued, forgiveness also entails a closure to history. Such closure both disclaims the immediate indebtedness of the guilty towards the victimised and frees the present and the future from the very burden of history's continual judgement that is the core of resistant form. Without that burden, remembrance will evaporate into oblivion and the same story of abusive power may recur as if for the first time. Hence Salma's wounds will not heal and rather than pardon, she will keep on reminding the guilty of what they are. In terms of Walcott's "truly tough aesthetic", history is not forgiven, and, in terms of Njabulo Ndebele's epitomisation of resistant form, the past offers a "moral foundation on which the future can be built".

Finally *The Ibis Tapestry* also resists its own form to a much larger degree than Serote does in his novel. Whereas *Gods of Our Time* includes no more than an indication of self-interrogation, in Moses' recognition that the task of passing on an idea of the people in the struggle is next to insurmountable and his acquiescence that his is far from the full story, *The Ibis Tapestry* ends with a sceptical reference to the entire project of narrativising history. Salma's appeal to the enduring weight of history is immediately countered by Poley's expression of a bleak but very contemporary inability to sense history: "The point is that, for the most part, history leaves me vacant. I can't imagine it" (200). He surrenders to apathy when thinking of the Holocaust, and, needless to say, the domestic holocaust of apartheid atrocities, admitting that he cannot "feel the suffering":

> ...I could remind myself: you are here to imagine an atrocity in order to keep it from being forgotten. You are here to imagine the deaths of the three girls and the wounding of Salma. You are here to imagine how at another city, the city of Damascus, four virgins were speared to death and their bodies pinioned to the city's wall. You are here to imagine why Christo Mercer chose this as his metaphor. But I couldn't (200-1).

This apathetic capacity may of course be read as an example of the forces of amnesia that Salma opposes. But then Poley also explains that he has trouble separating reality from fiction. When he watches Nazi documentaries of "Germans machine-gunning the village men, loading the women into cattle trucks", he has to remind himself that this actually happened as it seems too much like any other war movie (199-200). As his ex-wife diagnoses: "Your trouble, Robert, is that the only real stuff going on in your head...is fiction. You can't see the world we live in" (200). Accordingly, the idea of intermixing fiction with history, although not rejected (as even hard facts like a piece of the Berlin Wall leave him detached (200)), is nevertheless problematised. After all, historical fiction may contribute to the confusion of what is deadly serious and what is kitsch, entertainment, or, for that matter, farcical parody. Consequently, Nicol desists from any pretence of enjoying an unchallengeable authority to represent the past.

Nicol's self-critical endnote may lead us on to some of the other setbacks of postmodern strategies. Antjie Krog, in one of *her* self-interrogating moments, mentions two of these. Textuality, she says, may be "wrenching the heart out of the horror" and "have no more than academic relevance". Certainly dry and bloodless textuality stands as an antitheses to Serote's elicitation of lived experience. As such there may be a difficulty in postmodernism of evoking in the reader any emotional attachment to the protagonist which generates the kind of sympathy that may prove to be decisive for the individual's cultivation of remembrance at the end of the day. If that is true, Nicol may have chosen a literary strategy that has a potential of undermining the whole objective of writing against forgetting.

At any rate, and this pertains to the second problem identified by Krog, postmodernism places a great responsibility of interpretation on the reader. To understand the ideas of textuality and intertextuality requires a certain degree of literary familiarity. Hence, as even Hutcheon admits, there is "a real threat of elitism or lack of access in the use of parody in any art. This question of accessibility is undeniably part of the politics of postmodern representation" (Hutcheon, 1989: 105). And in South Africa with its third world illiteracy rate and an ignominious history of "Bantu education", the politics of elitism in postmodern art is probably the greatest impediment for Nicol in conveying his views on a wider scale. (For the incapacitating effects of Bantu education see Ndebele, 1994: 25-7).

As is evident when contrasting *Gods of Our Time* with *The Ibis Tapestry*, there is in South African historical fiction a simultaneous search for both a literature that may convey a sense of lived experience of the past and a literature that may issue in its own terms in rivalry with the discourse of historical writing. It may be argued that the gap between Serote and Nicol in this respect is filled by the magical realism of Mda's *Ways of Dying*[10]. In fact many critics refer to magical realism as a form that places itself in-between realism and postmodernism. On the one hand, the fusion of the real with the fantastic serves to perform tricks on reality and to disrupt the normative epistemology of scientific rationality and historical linearity (Faris, 1995: 163, 167-8). Like postmodernism, magical realism thus frees literature from its traditional mimetic role and subverts our meaning-making systems (Zamora and Faris, 1995: 5-6). On the other hand, magical realism shares with realism the detail and concreteness of descriptions of the world we live in (Faris, 1995: 169-70). So, in spite of its association with postmodernism's assault on monological ways of perceiving and representing the world, magical realism is an effective strategy in summoning the sense of felt history that is present in Serote and may appear lacking in Nicol. Compared to Nicol's theoretical and abstract approach to his historical material, the realist ingredient in *Ways of Dying* ensures a much more empirical gateway to history in which the past is pictured with immediate and candid clarity. In this case, then, magical realism manages to contribute to history an appreciation of lived experience while at the same time avoiding the subordination of the historical novel to the conventional discourse of history. Finally, after the explorations into the European traditions of natural realism and postmodernism with the just mentioned elitist implications in the latter, magical realism offers a possibility of literary homecoming to the African continent.

The following interpretation of *Ways of Dying* is informed by all the above views. Moreover, it will be shown how the novel exemplifies the final layer in a holistic view of history in the sense that it represents history as the future. Whereas Serote explores history as the past in his presentation of the struggle and Nicol explores history as the present in his interrogation of the contemporary discussion of how to remember, Zakes Mda's use of history implies several visions of the South Africa to come. After a brief consideration of the metaphorical set-up and a juxtaposition of the historical versus the literary modules of the novel, it will be shown how Zakes Mda at once implies a possible promise of the future as well as a serious admonition. It will be argued that Mda, in order for the future promise to come true, calls for cultural empowerment of the people to support the political empowerment Serote is concerned with, and that he supplies Nicol's preoccupation with contrition with a demand for material redistribution.

In contrast to the thematisation in Serote and Nicol of the actors within the struggle movement and its oppressive counterpart, the events in *Ways of Dying*, despite several characters' engagement in the resistance, unfold from that still veiled margin of South Africa, the voiceless people living in the tin shacks of the "shanty towns", the "squatter camps" or the "informal settlements" – whichever term sounds the most or the least agreeable.

# Zakes Mda: *Ways of Dying*

All the historical elements in *Ways of Dying* evolve from the story of two village cousins, Noria and Toloki, who meet again in adulthood after a long spell of separation; both having been away from home and having led their lives independently since adolescence. Gradually, as they confide in each other about their pasts, a picture emerges of two different, but rather emblematic, lives torn by the course of South African history. Both protagonists left the countryside to seek their fortunes in the city, only to be sucked into a whirlpool of squalor, rejection, dejection and violence. Toloki, as a result, has retreated to a hermetic life of homelessness after an elapse of abuse and ostracism and Noria has lost the magical powers she possessed back in the village of evoking happiness around her with her laughter and song. She has turned into an empty shell after a failed marriage, prostitution and the loss of two sons of whom the latter is said to have been the reincarnation of the former. The first son, Vutha, was chained to a pole by his father and died of starvation. The second son, Vutha the Second, whose father is unknown, is executed by the liberation movement, accused of being an informer of the rival ethnic group, despite his age of five.

As Noria and Toloki reacquaint themselves with each other and fall in love, they learn to combine their strengths, revived from their creative minds and innocent fascination with life, to vindicate ways of living despite the life-negating realities of squatter camp existence and the prevalence of the violence and destruction that pervade their surroundings.

With *Ways of Dying*, we stay within recent South African history. The narrative time, although vague through the absence of any specific reference to time and place, can be identified as the transition years of the early 1990s. Notably, the historical focus is on the problems of violence that spilled over into the transition from the South

Africa of the 1980s that Serote and Nicol characterise. Instead of a relief from violence with the beginning of negotiations between the warring factions, the country seemed on the brink of disintegrating into a hellish scenario of uncompromising racial and ethnic antagonism, arbitrary killings and pervasive lawlessness. This is illustrated in Mda with the historical accuracy and biting realism we saw in Serote. Clashes between youth and police continue and *tsotsis* and state-sponsored vigilantes are savaging train commuters and the townships relentlessly. The Third Force continues its covert tyranny, supplemented by an upsurge in right-wing assaults on random black victims. And ethnic violence, orchestrated by the apartheid police force and spearheaded by Mangosuthu Buthelezi (alluded to in the story as "the tribal chief"), is threatening to plunge the country into a bloody civil war (17, 169, 170, 88-9, 132-34). The latter is evidently an expression of the fear that was generated by the death tolls in ethnic hostilities which amounted to 6.000 in the years between 1990 and 1995 (Maphai, 1995: 73).

However, the tropes that run through the novel to capture the essence of this society imaginatively are surprisingly ambivalent, wavering, as Johan van Wyk observes, between the apocalyptic and the carnivalesque (van Wyk, 1997: 80). The apocalyptic revolves around an imagery of all-consuming death that spreads from the war between the state and its resistance, to the killing of children and the killing of birth itself. The final stage represents the doom of halted fertility and is referred to symbolically on several occasions. It is followed through in the images of murders of innocent children, of men being forced to make love to corpses, and it culminates in the symbolic scene at the massacre in the squatter camp by the police and tribal agitators where a pregnant woman is stabbed with a spear. In the minutes before she dies, her labour begins, but as soon as the baby's head appears it is chopped off (170). "Soon we shall experience the death of birth itself", is the germane reaction to the whole situation when the funeral orator, the "nurse", is obituarising Noria's second son, the reincarnation of her first child, on the birthday of Christ at the beginning of the novel (5). If fecundity is squelched, the only thing that is given life is death. At another funeral, of a father who was murdered at his son's funeral, the nurse closes the circle of national self-destruction: "funerals acquire a life of their own, and give birth to other funerals" (149).

The carnivalesque interrupts to offer a strange but welcome relief to the otherwise grim picture. Whereas the apocalyptic images suggest death-in-life, the relief is to be found in its antonymic coinage life-in-death, as a whole range of examples confirm the presence of a courageous spirit in the face of death. These reveal themselves as an element of comedy that fuses with times of deadly seriousness. At one point several funeral parties fill the entire cemetery with laughter as the nurse at one of the graves passes a joke about the deceased. Likewise the novel opens with slapstick humour, when the funeral procession of Noria's son collides with a merry wedding procession; and a comedy of errors evolves when two bodies are mistakenly swopped in a morgue (152-3, 7, 17). But the components of life-in-death run deeper than mere comedy.

A notable manifestation of the carnivalesque is in the character of Toloki who himself encompasses the dual representation of thanatos and libido. Since childhood he has always been associated with death-in-life. Growing up in the village, he was treated cruelly as a social outcast. People regarded him as ugly with the looks of "something that has come to fetch us from the other world" (64). The strong link with the other world is maintained in his adult life. He establishes himself as a professional funeral mourner in the city and apart from being referred to by others as smelling of death (50, 90), he forges the otherworldly connexion himself by stating that "death continues every day. Death becomes me, it is part of me" (106). Yet his professional costume evokes as much of the burlesque as solemnity in relation to his vocation. Bought a long time ago in a shop that rented out strange and fanciful costumes for parties, Toloki's all-black scarecrow outfit with tight pants, cape and top hat (21), is evocative, as van Wyk points out, of New Year carnivals as much as of the terror of Halloween: death is contextualised with the games and fun of imagination (van Wyk, 1997: 88). In addition, Toloki is one of the most zealous characters in the novel. Notwithstanding his solemn companionship with the dead, the principle of life-in-death is expressed in both his witty allusions to his austere occupation as well as in the fact that he makes a living out of other people's mortality. As he puts it: "As long as there are funerals I'll survive" (46).

The ambivalence thus surrounding the representation of the country's violent history will be explained in this analysis by, once again, turning to the two functions of literature identified by Njabulo Ndebele. To recount what has been said about Ndebele so far, he operates with literature as a medium that may inform as well as involve its readers; literature may serve to display a recognisable picture of reality, or history, and it may serve to bring about a transformation of reader consciousness. Although the latter appears as the nobler purpose in Ndebele's criticism, in that it contributes to the development of such human preferences as sensitivity, subtlety and critical insight on which the perfection of any society depends, and although Ndebele has criticised resistance literature for being superficially sensationalist because its authors were preoccupied with informing without involving, both functions of literature must be regarded as relevant (see Ndebele, 1994: 40-53, 73).

Translating the mentioned doublesidedness in Mda's representation of the past into Ndebele's terminology, it is arguable that the very realistic and uncompromising depiction of violence and its metaphorical support in the apocalyptic strand of the novel corresponds to Ndebele's notions of supplying the reader with a recognisable reality. Mda seeks to communicate a picture of the violence of the past with an imagery and a realism that is as palpable as that in Serote where the unpleasantness of the past is to be mirrored in no uncertain terms. Conversely, the carnivalesque involves the reader by inviting a change of consciousness, not unlike Lindi's song in *Gods of Our Time*, that may result in socially and culturally constructive ways of dealing with an otherwise malignant past. These two sides to the novel will be followed through in turn. To start off with the informative presentation of history, Mda provides the reader with a familiar picture of how several dynamics have contributed to a particularly harsh brutalisation of the people of the country's social periphery, all leading to a state of social, cultural and moral dislocation in the novel's present.

As Toloki and Noria re-familiarize themselves with each other, we are provided with a multitude of flashbacks and digressions from the main story that explain how the present came to be through a dismembering past of western intrusion and apartheid tyranny. Already in their youth, the stronger forces of western modernisation begin to make themselves felt in the violent clashes between old and new value systems. Competition arises between traditional religion and Christianity, embodied respectively in Noria's mother, That Mountain Woman, who works as a *sangoma* and in the Archbishop's independent church (96-7). Similarly, Napu, Noria's lover, is enabled by the opportunity of wage labour to acquire a status of individual independence and break loose from the traditional system of bride wealth liability towards the family-in-laws. Instead of paying *lobola*, he takes the pregnant Noria away to get married before the magistrate (69). Lured by the bright lights, they seek their fortune in the promises of the new values of the city. But the promises, of course, turn out to be illusory: "There were no diamonds", Noria relates, "nor was there gold. Only mud and open sewers" (126). Napu is not able to provide for his wife and son and their marriage sinks with the material and spiritual deprivation of their lives. The final stage of bereavement is reached when Noria prostitutes herself in order to survive. As she sums it up bleakly herself: "I have been chewed, Toloki. Chewed and then spewed" (135). When we meet her again in the squatter camp, she has lost the magical laughter that evoked immediate happiness around her in the distant time and place of the village. Libido has been reduced to a faint will merely to stay alive.

Toloki follows the same path from a traditional rural past to the disillusion of modernisation, although his passage is qualitatively different from Noria's. Whereas the story of Noria illustrates the social and cultural uprooting of black South Africa, Toloki's delineates the moral disintegration of the apartheid society into a chaos of callous violence. He flees the village after having been brutally assaulted by his father but his ensuing quest for "love and fortune" is "dogged by deaths and funerals throughout" (58). From the countryside, where white farmhands set alight their black colleagues for the fun of it and a whole community abominates itself by cruelly murdering ten bandits in a moment of raging mass-justice, he moves to the city where death and apathy are "even more plentiful", as described at the beginning of this analysis (57). Life has become worthless as apartheid and its multiple consequences breed an inferno of obduracy, abuse and anarchy. In the words of a nurse:

> Normal deaths are those deaths that we have become accustomed to, deaths that happen everyday. They are deaths of the gun, and the knife, and torture and gore. We don't normally see people who die of illness or of old age (146-7).

This remark seems closely coupled with the central phrase of the novel which touches on the self-enforcing catalyst of social, cultural and moral depravity:

> Death lives with us everyday. Indeed our ways of dying are our ways of living. Or should I say our ways of living are our ways of dying? (89).

The normality of murder, torture and gore referred to by the nurse further contaminates the already bleak ways of living, which in turn precipitates more death in an endless vicious circle. It is the sign of a prideless society that has turned in on itself in a thrust of self-destruction where even innocence kills and is killed. As in the case of Vutha the Second who is necklaced by the youth of the resistance movement and set alight by his playmate (177).

The sociologist Dumisane Ngcobo, in addressing the social, cultural and moral upheaval that has been sketched in the realist strand of Mda's novel, speaks of an aftermath of nihilism, mass psychological depression and social despair among large sections of the black South African community (Ngcobo, 1999: 139). Their willing or forced acceptance of alien Eurocentric worldviews in the modernisation process has resulted in Africans being de-centred to the fringes of a basically European civilisation. This denigration, Ngcobo goes on, "is carried out through a denial of blacks of their own history and thus a denial of their humanity..." (140). To further explicate Ngcobo's contention, non-western people in their representation in Eurocentric discourse is characterised by their "lessness". According to Frantz Fanon, Eurocentric discourse has pervaded every sphere of life in the postcolonial world as a legacy of colonialism. African children, for example, are brought up to see the world from an almost exclusively Western perspective. The education they receive is European through and through. Even entertainment is produced in the west, with Tarzan or Crusoe against the savage world as the archetypal hero-villain structure. Western bias is stigmatised even on word level to impose itself on consciousness: black is "evil", "dirty", "diabolic"; white is "innocent", "bright", "clean", "pure" (Fanon, 1967: 189). From childhood, black identity is thus subconsciously subordinated, or "socially appropriated", in Foucaultian terms, by the endless reproduction of the European ideal (Fanon, 1967: 146-9 and Foucault, 1972: 227). Transferred to Jackson's theories on storytelling, such representation is devastating to self-perception. Drawing on Jean-Paul Sartre's observations, he states that shame and self-negation arise

> ...when the recognition of who one is ceases to be mirrored by those one loves, and comes to be determined by one's appearance in the eyes of others, filled with indifference or hate.... [A]ny inner reflections on *who* one is are eclipsed by the external definition of *what* one is in the eyes of others. No longer a subject for-oneself, one is reduced to being an object – isolated, exposed, fixed, categorised, and judged by the Other (Jackson, 2002: 58).

In South Africa, Ngcobo says, the imposition of alien and rather self-centred norms and world views at the expense of a culturally imbedded value system coupled with the undermining of society by violence have entailed "a near eclipse of hope and collapse of meaning" (141). Certainly this has long been the state of affairs in the squatter camps depicted by Mda, which have remained a monument of economic exploitation and socio-cultural ostracism ever since Toloki acquainted himself with them eighteen years ago (138).

Against such circumstances of absolute public and private self-negation, the only remedy, says Ngcobo, is "a new black leadership grounded in African culture and capable of removing the defeatist attitude from amongst the black periphery" (153). In other words, a self-generated discourse is needed in which people are allowed to fashion a positive self-image and are allowed the necessary amount of autonomy of the definition of reality it takes to influence and to change reality.

This is precisely where the second, the consciousness-raising element of Mda's fiction sets in. Whereas a recognisable picture of the South African transition and the socio-cultural causes that lead up to its dismal disposition represent the historical thread in the novel, the aforementioned life-in-death qualities run as a strong ahistoric or imagined undercurrent of the narration. As in the case of Serote's psychological probe into the consciousness of the struggle and Lindi's song, the imagined domain supplies the historical information with a conjectural vestige of how to counteract the historical reality. As in Serote, creativity plays a crucial role in dignifying the ways of living and dying in the face of ugliness and abomination. Indeed Toloki and Noria, in drawing, singing and in their artistic construction of Noria's tin shack, manage to humanise the most inhuman conditions. The shack, in their eyes, becomes a piece of art and it is the power of imagination, too, that enables them to "see beauty where there is none" in the scene where the couple transcend the depressing reality of their surroundings by envisioning another, prettier world with comforts and a garden on the walls papered with bright pictures cut from glossy magazines (103-4). However, in contrast to Serote, the consciousness-raising mechanisms in Mda's novel are much more concerned with an explicitly cultural revival, as if responding directly to Albie Sach's request in 1989 for a development of an "artistic and cultural vision" that corresponds to the political development of South Africa" (Sachs, 1998: 239). To elaborate briefly on Ndebele's literary theory, he agrees with Ngcobo that cultural recuperation among the oppressed in South Africa is essential in rejuvenating a sense of social positivism. He qualifies the literature of involvement as a literature that frees the social and cultural imagination, to reconstruct an African aesthetic and value system after the disruptions caused by European hegemony:

> The material life of Africans should be given a new forward articulation that will enlarge intellectual interest and expand the possibilities of imagination. It is a re-evaluation which, I believe, should result in a profound philosophical transformation of the African consciousness, a consciousness that should and must endure (Ndebele, 1994: 161).

Mda returns to the same idea in his visions for the genre that has earned him his renown, the Theatre for Development, by proposing that "…Development is meaningful only if it allows for the empowerment of local communities…to promote a spirit of self-reliance among the marginalised" (quoted in Mervis, 1998: 39). In this respect creative works play the crucial role of "enrich[ing] and expand[ing] people's own forms of expression". A play or a piece of literature thereby "strengthens the point of view of the most progressive section of the people; and it roots itself in tradition and develops this in a positive manner" (quoted in Mervis, 1998: 44). As it has been shown, Serote does move beyond the stage of mere informing to involve the reader in a scrutiny of the psychological depth of subjugation. However, in spite of his own appeal in an interview to rearticulate the "wisdoms, gems and treasures of African culture", there is little of this in *Gods of Our Time*, apart from in Lindi's song at the end (Solberg, 1998: 84). Conversely, the theme of life-in-death in *Ways of Dying*, the ways of living, that particularly Toloki and Noria are searching for, is often intricately associated with an attempt to reconnect themselves with a humanist value system that, to a large extent, is rooted in the African tradition they were born into. Another way of putting this is that Serote's preoccupation with political empowerment is shifted in Mda to a preoccupation with social and cultural empowerment. And in a manner of speaking, the absence of a survival language in Serote's characters, and the tentative suggestions of its recovery in a self-reliant form of expression, is to be found in Mda in the explicit reconnection of life with African tradition and ethos.

Hence, a version of the Ubuntu philosophy is to be found in the squatter camp community which is surviving history on mutual caring and assistance, generosity and selflessness (42-3, 60-2, 125-6). Moreover, values are frequently drawn from pools of traditional wisdom. Proverbs, for instance, soothe people not to despair by the burden of hardship: "Our elders say", Toloki is reminded by Noria, "that an elephant does not find its own trunk heavy" and "In our language there is a proverb which says the greatest death is laughter" (157 and 153). Likewise there is the reassurance of tradition in the metaphor of Toloki and Noria's way of sleeping. According to custom, they curl up in a foetal position, thus suggesting the auspicious quality of shared cultural values. Not only do they reassure the community a sense of togetherness and belonging, they produce a promise of life and regeneration, signalled in the connotations of the unborn child and rebirth every morning that may be affirmed even in the midst of death and destruction. In that light, the coinage "Our ways of dying are our ways of living" and "our ways of living are our ways of dying", becomes positively ambivalent by also inviting a change of consciousness that diminishes the weight of affliction. It becomes possible to humanise the ways of dying, if the ways of living are generated from the larger body of the community as well as from the accumulation of knowledge and experience that is expressed through its cultural idioms. Or, to contextualise the central lines with Ndebele, the transformation of consciousness, from that of self-destruction to regeneration, relies on "a forward articulation" of "African social and cultural consciousness".

At a metanarrative level, the novel itself underscores the urge to overcome "the defeatist attitude" among black South Africans that Ngcobo speaks of in that several formal strategies are adopted to articulate an African aesthetic. First of all there is the narrative voice. The narrators, the plural "we", explicitly assign their authority to the oral tradition:

> Just like back in the village, we live our lives together as one. We know everything about everybody. We even know things that happened when we were not there.... We are the all-seeing eye of the village gossip. When in our orature the storyteller begins the story, 'They say it happened...' we are the 'they'. No individual is the owner of the story. The community is the owner of the story, and it can tell it the way it deems it fit. We would not be needing to justify the communal voice that tells this story if you had not wondered how we became so omniscient in the affairs of Toloki and Noria (8).

In this way the indigenous techniques of story telling are foregrounded in the otherwise alien form of the written novel and the western literary concept of the "omniscient narrator" is amusingly concretized by constituting a participatory, physical presence in the story.

The structure of the narration shares similar features from orature. The main storyline digresses with flashbacks of other stories in what Margaret Mervis calls a "disjunctive style" which, she says, "negates linear time, reflecting rather the cyclical nature of oral narrative" (Mervis, 1998: 50). One may even elaborate on Mervis' observation and argue that the time structure of *Ways of Dying* is spiral more than cyclical. The return to the trope of rebirth at the end of the novel, for example, where Toloki and Noria wake up on New Year's Day from sleeping naked in the foetal position, has been pushed in a positive or upward direction in comparison with the starting point of the narrative circle on Christmas Day (9, 181-2).

The renewal of life implied at the end of the novel is not shaded by the burial of new life as it is at its beginning and likewise the still burning tyres at the New Year celebrations, which carry the connotations of necklacing and the killing of Vutha, release only the smell of "pure wholesome rubber" without "the sickly stench of roasting human flesh" (199).

Thirdly, Mda's application of the English language invites the imposition of local mastery of the foreign medium. As mentioned in the analysis of *The Ibis Tapestry*, language, to Bakhtin, is "overpopulated with the intentions of others". The implications of this propagation are but aggravated when the value-laden language is that of a former coloniser with a long history of subordinating indigenous modes of expression. In the face of this, Mda overcomes the stigmatisation in the master language of otherness and subordination by adapting English to a local colour. The text which is richly interspersed with African proverbs, expressions and idioms, comprises an altogether African South African English (see: 3, 6, 22, 56, 68). Against this background it is arguable that Achmat Dangor misses the mark when he in his harsh critique of *Ways of Dying* dismisses Mda's language as "laboured" and proliferated with "badly constructed sentences and malapropisms" (Dangor, 1996: 22). In fact any interest in standardising English in accord with metropolitan dictum is bound to be outvoiced in the future South Africa. Hitting the nail on the head, Guy Butler predicts that "twenty million blacks will use English for their own interests and ends, without worrying much about the views of less than two million English-speaking South Africans" (quoted in Ndebele, 1994: 99).

In inseparable closeness to Ndebele's twin paradigms of a consciousness-raising literature and the revival of African culture is, of course, the embrace in Mda's novel of magical realism. Magical realism itself is, as Michael Chapman has aptly demonstrated, an integral part of African orature in which "imagination conjures up a plentitude of possibility in the emotion-saturated, surprising language of dream and desire" (Chapman, 1996: 48 and 40-9). At the same time there is in magical realism, as an independent contemporary form, an inherent appeal to the validity of traditional cosmologies, which only reinforces its faculty for cultural revival. According to Gabrielle Foreman, Magical realism bypasses what may seem as the "total negation of faith and tradition" in modern civilisation. Magical realism, she says:

> ...presumes that the individual requires a bond with the traditions and the faith of the community, that s/he is historically constructed and connected. Echoing Alejo Carpentier, who first named the phenomenon, critic Marguerite Suárez-Murias contends that 'the marvellous...presupposes an element of faith on the part of the author or the audience' (Foreman, 1995: 286).

Hence a connection is drawn between gusto and the traditional past, as in the metaphor of the figurines made by Toloki's father Jwara which bring bliss and amusement to the children of the squatter camp at the end of the novel (197-8). The figurines were created by an amalgamation of two forces, Noria's magical singing and Jwara's dreams (23, 25). Bearing in mind that dreams in African oral tradition are often associated with messages from ancestors (see van Wyk, 1997: 83), there is a promise of restored placidity, symbolised in the township children's laughter, by cultivating a creative link between the traditions of the past and the present. The figurines, it should be noted, too, are brought to the squatter camp by the otherwise anaemic undertaker Nefodolodwhe whose financial success has made him discard all connections with his "backward" and "indolent" people. At one point, his westernized consciousness recedes as he is forced to make a tribute of recognition towards his kinsmen after Jwara's ghost has haunted him with the demand that he find the figurines in the village and return them (189-94). The magic that is offered in African folklore also helps Noria surmount the tyrannical presence of history in a much more subtle, and perhaps for that reason a much more successful and convincing way. After her first son, Vuthi, falls victim to the state of depravity that is forced upon the squatter camp environment, in that he is kidnapped by his morose father and dies tied to a pole without food and water, it is through the magic of divine conception and reincarnation that she overcomes the loss (139-40). Whether the magic is to be interpreted as ontological, as reality being magic, or epistemological, as Noria's worldview being magic, the fact remains that her African heritage tenders an alternative reality that defiantly slips through the claws of history (for ontological and epistemological magic see Faris, 1995: 165)[11].

At this stage it is appropriate to insert the caveat that Mda, despite his emphasis on cultural self-determination, does not present an uncritical embrace of African tradition or advocate a new form of cultural chauvinism in South Africa. As it is, he incorporates in the novel a resistance to its own form. This is primarily expressed in the narrative voice which, on the one hand, is self-critical of the community it represents and, on the other, not always reliable. In regard of the sexual escapades of That Mountain Woman (who is from another village), the narrators say: "We told the story over and over again, and we laughed and we said, 'That Mountain Woman has no shame'". After which it is confessed: "But one could detect a smack of envy in our voices when we said that. Those were adventures that would never be seen in our conservative village" (34). As concerns the cruel treatment by the community of Toloki in his childhood who would mercilessly be chased away for his ugliness when everybody enjoyed Noria's laughter, the unreliability of the narrators reveals itself when they claim always to have been happy when Toloki and Noria were happy and felt the pain when they were hurt (8)[12]. Instead, the cultural regeneration that Mda offers, is to evolve from a non-essentialist and non-static dialogue between the values of tradition and contemporary needs and as long as Africans recover from the defeatist attitude about their own tradition, the ideal of hybridising African culture with all other cultures in South Africa is not rejected. This idea is in many ways illustrated in Toloki's vocation which is soundly rooted in and in touch with traditional African practices, yet greatly inspired and moulded by so many other cultures and religions, from Hinduism to Christianity (see 125)[13]. Similarly it has been shown how the novel itself forms a great hybrid between a modern, western tradition and African traditions of storytelling.

In addition to the culturally transformative elements that have been analysed, the insertion of magical realism into a historical novel may also be interpreted in terms of Coetzee's notions of a literature in rivalry with the discourse of history. Accordingly, it is the argument here that *Ways of Dying*, in addition to applying to Ndebele's theory of a literature informing and involving, reaches beyond the kind of supplementary historical fiction that merely adds to history a certain density of observation or lived experience[14]. Just as the magic fences off the tyrannical presence of history in Noria's story of divine conception, the tyrannical presence of the discourse of history is fenced off by magical realism as a creative mode in assertion of an entirely independent literary discourse.

The fusion of magic with reality in the novel, such as Noria's second pregnancy or Toloki's ability to remember his father's death before he has heard of it (van Wyk, 1997: 101), is as disruptive of the conventional discourse of history with its foundations in western rationality and logic as Nicol's deconstruction of narrative authority and objectivity. And like Nicol's postmodern ventures, the magic in *Ways of Dying* opens up another discursive universe distinct from that of the traditional historical novel insofar as it offers an alternative epistemology, in oxymoronic rivalry with the historical material that is presented. In this respect, Faris and Zamora claim that:

> ...magical realism is a mode suited to exploring – and transgressing – boundaries, whether the boundaries are ontological, political, geographical or generic. Magical realism often facilitates the fusion, or coexistence, of possible worlds, spaces, systems that would be irreconcilable in other modes of fiction. The propensity of magical realist texts to admit a plurality of worlds means that they often situate themselves on laminal territory between or among those worlds – in phenomenal and spiritual regions where transformation,

> metamorphosis, dissolution are common, where magic is a branch of naturalism, or pragmatism (5-6).

In other words, Mda is able to set up a parallel discourse of promise that coexists ahistorically with and in rivalry to the historical discourse, the realism, of the novel. Whereas the discourse of history and rationality, employed in the novel's realistic representations of history, offers only a bleak life-negating predictability of cause and effect gathering a momentum of misery, the elements of the fantastic explode the confines of that very discourse by inviting us, like *The Ibis Tapestry*, to *think* differently from the dominant meaning-making systems. Only with another language of extended possibilities does it become feasible to deal with and thus to counteract the course of history. Hence multiple historical causes effect the death of Noria's son, but magic brings him back to her; multiple historical forces turn Nefodolodwhe against his own people, but magic, the return of Jwara's ghost in his dreams, forces him to reconnect: and multiple historical forces sentence Noria and Toloki to a squalid existence and also deprive Noria of her second child, but magic, or at least epistemological magic, conjures up another mindset between the two of them that helps them conquer these realities. The discourse of magic, to sum up, defies the inevitable defeat that permeates the discourse of history. The mode of loss is countered with a mode of replenishment.

A question that comes to mind when considering the depiction of suffering in *Ways of Dying* is whether the blend of carnivalesque and magical ingredients does not diminish the drabness of the realism. One argument that may be launched against the aesthetic elements in the novel is definitely that beauty may take the sting out of suffering and consequently erode the political message of calling attention to the injustice committed against the destitute in South Africa, then as well as now. The beauty that Toloki and Noria are able to conjure out of their drab reality, for example, as well as magical realism itself, could foster an unintentional romanticization of the squatter camps where a hard-hitting realism would have had an uncompromising effect. However, as André Brink argues, creativity and imagination are in many instances required to make suffering palpable. As a sobering contrast, Brink calls attention to the mind-numbing effect of the persistent realistic reportage of violence on television, which was also what inhibited Poley in *The Ibis Tapestry* (Brink, 1998: 19-21). In alignment with Brink's argument, it may be maintained that it is not sheer beauty but a certain *tragedy* in the beauty, when, for example, Toloki and Noria wander in their imagined and materially unobtainable garden. This generates a sense of deflation lurking right below the surface of the thrill of the moment. Similarly it is the duality in the book of history and the human responses that makes us recognise at one and the same time the inhumanity of life in the squatter camps and the humanity of those bawdy, miserable people who are so easily dehumanised.

In further accord with Brink's contention, many critics share the conviction that magical realism may be seen as "an antidote to the exhausted forms of expression", such as natural realism and postmodernism (Zamora and Faris, 1995: 7). So the ambiguous representation of the past in *Ways of Dying*, which simultaneously confirms a well-known picture of reality and disrupts our normative perceptions of reality, enforces on the reader a new and fresh engagement with the history before him or her. In other words, it provokes an attention-drawing and, with its metaphorical potency, consciousness-raising actuality, which urges the centre of society to reconsider its derisive perception of the periphery.

To return briefly to the constellations in the novel between the discourse of history and the discourse of literature, these become all the clearer when *Ways of Dying* is interpreted as a future history. Whereas the historical material in the novel represents a world of facts, the counter-historical discourse of magic represents a world of utopian longings. Michael Green maintains that in contrast to historians who are reluctant or unwilling to make predictions about the future:

> ...novelists are precisely able to ignore the caution of the historian because their enterprise carries, quite obviously, a different emphasis. Their concern is to make the present meaningful in terms of its possible outcome; the imaginative effort invested in this is not to be measured in terms of their literal ability correctly to foresee the outcome, but rather in their ability to use a particular literary strategy to intervene in the present (257-8).

Accordingly the magical realist components of *Ways of Dying* disrupt the discourse of history, that so blatantly mirrors poor South Africans in a world of denial and destruction, and offer instead a discourse of opportunity by means of which the dystopian direction of history can be changed to a utopian direction. At the same time, it is arguable that the capacity of magical realism for disrupting our normative perceptions of reality is a prerequisite for the change of consciousness it takes to acknowledge the utopian allusions of the novel as other than outrageous. In Coetzeean terms of a rival aesthetic, the magical universe in *Ways of Dying* and its utopian implications empower the novel to "evolve its own paradigms" and "issue its own terms", independently of the discourse of history, in a way that forces upon us a reassessment of what is considered socially, politically and economically plausible. In the words of André Brink, we are urged to:

> ...imagine what has previously been impossible: to grapple, exuberantly and adventurously, with the limits of the possible.... [as] only by dreaming and writing the impossible can life be made possible (Brink, 1993: 2).

It is the utopian aspirations and their very probability in alternity which impinge themselves on present reality and keeps us in touch with the very sources of revolutionary energy in the midst of a worldwide supremacy of conservative politics (see also Jameson quoted in Green, 1997: 248-9).

With that, it is fitting to delve further into that Other historical discourse of the novel, off-limits to the ordinary historian, the implied visions of the future, which also come in other forms than the magical.

Green explains about future histories that they:

> ...seek to comment upon the past and present by projecting the implications of the past and the present forward in time. In this way they reverse the standard techniques of historical fiction, but remain directly related to them. In any event, attempts to give meaning to the past generally involve...an implied or explicit appeal to the future (244).

This appeal to the future, he continues, can involve either a desire or a warning, a utopia or a dystopia (264). As it has been indicated, history in Mda's novel contains a projection of both in correspondence with double entendre of the imagery; that of the carnivalesque and that of nightmarish terror.

To outline briefly the utopian allusions, which have already been suggested in the analyses of the consciousness-raising dynamics of the novel and its rival mode, there is a utopian desire embodied in Toloki, Noria and their good neighbours to overcome the burdens of the past by recreating a social fabric woven by moral, cultural, communal and humanist positivism. This will engender an all-inclusive society based on a shared set of values, including economic, racial and gender equality, social responsibility and pacifism. In short, a society constructed on a social conscience similar to the philosophy of Ubuntu that disallows any form of human abuse or undesirable marginalisation. As has also been stated, it is not only their political inferiority that Serote is concerned with, but the social and cultural deprivation of the majority of the South African population that must undergo resuscitative treatment, if they are to have any democratic right of independently participating in shaping society. Only then, says Ndebele, will the oppressed discover a "new, rich and very complex social language of their own" (1994: 119).

The dystopian indications in *Ways of Dying* evidently centre on the further disintegration of society into an anarchy of violence, civil war and utter self-destruction, if no counter is generated to stop it. The emphasis in the novel on the "tribal chief", for example, and his ability to animate an imagined and aggressive ethnicity warns of the destructive potential of group politics coupled with political intolerance and a zero-sum orientation (e.g. see 47-9). Similarly post-apartheid South Africa is experiencing a taste of the dystopian vision of the novel. Hein Marais, for instance, refers to the phenomenon of a "lost generation" of South African youth "with little education, poor job prospects, and prone – en masse, it seem[s] – to violence and other 'anti-social' behaviour" (110; see also Deegan, 1999: 173). The crime statistics speak for themselves: more than 20,000 South Africans were murdered in 1995 and 36,888 cases of rape or attempted rape were reported. The same year, there were 12,531 cases of vehicle hijackings and 1996 counted 481 crime syndicates operating in the country. Moreover, cases of burglary, robbery, assaults and drug trafficking in South Africa continue to hover among the highest numbers in the world (Marais, 1998: 107, 109). Again this can be contextualised with the disappearance of the enemy for the combat-minded youth in *Gods of Our Time* who, adding insult to injury, have no other skills than fighting and are offered no alternative livelihood.

Obviously the development of the spiritual culture of the country – intellectualism, ideas, feelings, ethics – to counter this dystopian advance is far from adequate to stop the tide of disintegration. There is a compelling need for the development of the material culture as well; for as long as scarcity exists for the masses, there is a breeding ground for animosities, be they based on race, class or ethnicity.

If navigated by utopian aspirations, post-apartheid South Africa will relieve the squatters of their material misery through economical redistribution. But *Ways of Dying* presents a past that is very prone to confer upon the country a drive in the direction of dystopia. First of all there is a brief mention of the rich whites at the tourist centre of the city who:

"don't pay any particular attention to [Toloki], except of course to make sure that their wallets and handbags are safe. But then that is what they do every time they see someone who does not look quite like them" (183).

In this snapshot description, superimposed on the background of the squatter camps, the entire question of future redistribution is encompassed. It points forward in time towards the indecisive resolution of the battle over South Africa, which has led Jay Reddy to comment that "the end of apartheid seems to represent for the white minority a defeat in which they have lost nothing" (quoted in Ndebele, 1994: 156). In other words, the negotiated settlement has guaranteed no material concessions on the side of the privileged for the sake of the underprivileged[15]. This is to be seen in the light that post-apartheid South Africa is still described by the World Bank as one of the most unequal economies in the world with a gini coefficient of no less than 0,68 (Marais, 1998: 106).

The implication of underlining the indifference of the rich to the poverty around them while not mentioning the question of guilt throughout the novel, seems, then, to agree with Ndebele when he, instead of guilt, demands that those who prospered on apartheid should accommodate the need for redistribution: "Guilt is irrelevant, but it crops up because the struggle was unresolved. Those who have lost should properly experience loss, not guilt" (156). Guilt, he goes on to say, is a personal flagellation that leads to humility which is not a good sight on a national scale. On the contrary, justice, understood as paying back, is a "decisive corrective action" that "leads to knowledge and responsibility". Although Mike Nicol in *The Ibis Tapestry* radically dismisses any alleviation of guilt for the sake of remembering, he shares with Ndebele and Mda the idea that the offenders are indebted to the offended, illustrated in Sarra's devotion to Salma's recovery. However, as was also shown in the analysis of *The Ibis Tapestry*, the *wealthy parts* of the white community are "ensconced in so much political and economical privilege" that they are able to barricade themselves and their riches behind barbed wired walls with "armed response" signs, from where it is easy to ignore the anguish of the periphery. Even if this may ultimately change the white phobia expressed in J. M. Coetzee's *Disgrace* of being "raped" through race-related retribution from a dormant to an actual peril.

There is also an appeal in *Ways of Dying* to the current incumbents. If the beneficiaries of apartheid are not ready to take direct responsibility, the initiative lies with the government. In this respect, the future African leadership is represented in a manner that may foretell rapture as well as agitation. It is a taste of utopia that the high-ranking leaders of the resistance movement visit absolutely the lowest end of the social scale to listen to their grievances. But the fact that the leaders arrive in a big, black Mercedes Benz, "high powered" and "bejewelled", already signals great distance (161-2). And aloofness is further emphasised when the leaders ask Noria, in perfect anticipation of the ANC's attempt to censor history as discussed in the Serote analysis, to keep silent about the execution of her son as it will weaken the outward image of the movement (166-7).

The question, then, is whether the leaders, once in power, will take the masses into consideration who bled for the common cause. Initially, the democratically elected government of 1994 set up the so-called Reconstruction and Development Programme for rapid redress of past inequalities, which, among other things, resulted in the extension of water and electricity supplies to many remote and poor areas of the country as well as the construction of one million houses. However, after less than two years, that ambitious programme was abandoned in favour of the current supply-side strategy, GEAR (Growth, Employment and Redistribution), that aims not at forthright redistribution, but at creating the most lucrative conditions for the private economy in the hope of bringing about a "trickle down effect" while cutting government spending and reducing state assets (Lundahl, 1998: 29-31). Similarly, there is clearly a government reluctance to implement even the recommendations of compensation and rehabilitation made by the Truth and Reconciliation Commission in its final report. The report suggests among other things that the beneficiaries of apartheid, and especially big business, should pay a reparations tax for the development of poor South Africa (see Krog, 1998: 432-3). As Annette Lansink says, none of the recommendations have materialised in government policy, and the funding of the Truth Commission's Reparations Committee is so severely curtailed that the majority of victims who were promised compensation are still waiting for it (Lansink, 2000: 9; see also Matlou, 2001 and Merten, 2001).

Above all the government and office holders appear more interested in careerism and in uniting the elite within the existing order rather than stirring up the masses with expectations of fast deliverance. Whatever it may be, it is certainly not the utopia embedded in Mda's history that dictates the direction of the near future in South Africa. The restraint in the country on the subject of social justice, among the privileged as among the government, is staggering when one considers the compelling and inescapable everyday signs of the wrongs of the past: the violence and the deprivation in the townships and squatter camps.

A third dimension that is included in Mda's future history of dystopia concerns the antithesis to the cultural flowering that was mentioned as part of the utopia. In the absence of a strong will to consciously develop independently along culturally connected lines, the alternative is an obdurate society of individuals bent on materialist self-gain. The representative of this future scenario is the undertaker Nefodolodwhe who has chosen an uncompromising denial of his rural past and developed an avaricious scavenger-mentality in looking forward to the fatal misfortune of his fellow men (see: 116-7).

Ndebele maintains that depriving the oppressed of any meaningful spiritual life of their own, as referred to earlier, has also deprived them of any control of their own fate. In correspondence with Ngcobo's argument that blacks have been denied their own history and humanity and Jackson's observations on discursive objectification, they are doomed to respond to history instead of initiating it (1994: 159). If this is not made up for, as in Mda's vision of a reaffirmation of African values, oppression will continue, although masked to the extent that the oppressed do not perceive their own oppression. The glitter of apartheid, Ndebele says, like materialistic extravagance, rich neighbourhoods, institutions of financial power, which previously represented exclusion and repulsive, exploitative white power, now represent "opportunity and possible fulfilment". And so the "brazen oppression of the past is now replaced with the seductive oppression of having to build and consolidate and enjoy what was achieved at our expense". Instead of a "self-created reality" the only option for the disempowered is then one of absorption and accommodation like Nefodolodwhe (153-4). Society will continue along the lines of the old order of the African being contained within a western pre-eminence rather than a new order of African self-determination in a truly free society. Instead of freedom, Ndebele concludes, spiritual emptiness will prevail at the expense of constructive content (136-7).

So, all in all, the past as it is represented in *Ways of Dying* contains a host of indications that point towards an undesirable future in South Africa and a continuation of the dystopian development that has gathered increasing impetus throughout the apartheid years and, earlier still, since the western disruption of the African civilisation. In order to turn the tide of historical cause and effect it is necessary, accordingly, to imagine the impossible. Hence the utopian innuendoes of a truly egalitarian society brought about by social and cultural self-determination are forwarded as an indismissable alternative, which, in the light of a discourse of expanded possibility, ought to appear all the less improbable.

# Resistant Form in *Ways of Dying*

So far Green's resistant form has been illustrated as the past passing judgement on the present, as in Serote's use of the past, and as the present passing judgement on itself, as in Nicol's use of the present as a historical moment of contention. With Mda it may be shown how the present may be judged by the future.

In Coetzee's *Dusklands*, the main character, S. J. Coetzee, turns our common idea of history upside down: "Man's thrust into the future is history; all the rest, the dallying by the wayside, the retraced path, belongs to anecdote, the evening by the hearth-fire" (quoted in Green, 1997: 235). Notwithstanding, the foregoing in *Ways of Dying* functions as more than sheer entertainment by the hearth-fire insofar as it is summoned to lunge us towards the future. To re-contextualise this with Coetzee, history is represented by Mda as the future through his implied visions of both promise and foreboding, and the contemporary use of the past functions as determinant of which direction the country will take.

In Jamesonian terms, the visions of promise and foreboding become points of judgement on the present:

> It is not only the past that judges us but the future as well [as] only the Utopian future is a place of truth…and the privilege of contemporary life and the present lies not in its possession, but at best in the rigorous judgement it may be felt to pass on us (quoted in Green, 1997: 31).

Elaborating on this, Michael Green goes on to locate future histories within the theory of resistant form as follows:

> If history…exists in its strongest form as a mode of resistance to the present (or the present to itself), then this utopian [or

dystopian] impulse – which is precisely a mode of resistance – takes on the shape of the historical in its relation to the moment of its production. Its strength depends upon the difference it is able to set up 'in the midst of all', 'against all that is'. It becomes the work of the future no less than the work of the past or the present in its oppositional sense to produce what...Jameson call[s]...the 'rigorous judgement' that is the real effect of powerfully told history; the future must remind us of 'what we are not yet' [or, in the dystopian mode, of what we risk becoming]. This it does by embodying within itself, positively or negatively displayed, the criteria by which to evaluate the present state of society (249-50).

The future, in other words, is held up before us to illuminate the deficiency of the social formation in which we exist and to warn against any wrong turn of development. In its quality of a utopian ideal, Jameson's "only place of truth", the future vision denies us any comfortable contentedness with the present state of affairs. And consequently we are sentenced by its merciless judgement to improve "all that is" in a continuous quest for the ideal. This is the function of utopia in *Ways of Dying*. As a future history, the novel sets up a Foucaultian difference, not unlike what we saw in Serote and Nicol, between the future and the present that challenges any claim that the struggle of South Africa ended with the democratic elections of 1994. The fulfilment of peacefulness, cultural self-determination, and general social and economic equality have not been reached with the end of apartheid and these comprise the ideals of "what we are not yet". Accordingly Mda resists the present in its uncritical embrace of the materialist glitter that continues, in Ndebele's terms, to enslave Africans to a non-African civilisation and excommunicates the majority of the South African population who do not have the preconditions, as pointed out by Ngcobo, for joining the modern competition of the survival of the fittest. He resists the forces in contemporary South Africa that are heading for an anaemic *Gesellschaft* rather than a human *Gemeinschaft*, insofar as he resists the scavenging "Nefodolodwhes" of the emerging African middle-class; the selfish protectionism of those who prospered on the exploitation of the previous dispensation; and the present government's leanings towards elitism in the midst of squatter camp destitution. For the same reasons, he resists the choice of the beneficiaries to barricade their riches rather than to fulfil their duty of social responsibility. If the present does not heed the judgement passed on it by the future as utopia, the dystopian implications in *Ways of Dying* warn of a perpetuation of the malaise of social fragmentation caused by ethnic, racial and class hostilities.

Yet to heed the rigorous judgement requires, in many instances, a change of consciousness. In that respect, it has been argued how the magical reality that breathes through the novel invites a change of consciousness that may surpass the modalities that are imposed on our habitual thinking by what we take for granted as logical and rational. Magical realism advances an alternative epistemology, and indeed an alternative ontology, in which the impossible, the belief in and the possibilities of utopias are not cast aside as ridiculously irrational in the manner of the discourse of political and economical liberalism. After all, it is utopia, and, in this context its probability in the mode of magical realism that, in Jameson's parallel to Brink, "keeps alive the possibility of a world qualitatively distinct from this one and takes the form of a stubborn negation of all that is", including our modes of thinking (quoted in Green, 1997: 248).

To move on to Green's notion of the future resistant form as constructed by "criteria by which to evaluate the present state of society", the immediate steps that Mda recommends be taken in the direction of utopia are quite tangible. In fact they may be summed up as supplementing and concretizing the central issues of *Gods of Our Time* and *The Ibis Tapestry*. The empowerment of the oppressed in altering the course of history that Serote indicates is conditioned in *Ways of Dying* by the ability of the oppressed to alter history not only on the political level but on the social and cultural level as well. In the same breath it should be repeated that *Ways of Dying* resists its own form by including a caution against a new form of social and cultural jingoism. African traditions should be revived not as a new rigorous version of cultural or racial purism, but as a rich language of positive self-definition that may freely enter into a constructive dialectic with other cultural strands in a world of endless change. And in regard to Mike Nicol's appeal to the responsibility of remembering and never disposing of the feeling of guilt, this will have no immediate significance in South Africa if it does not materialise in the concrete expiation of economic redistribution. South Africa cannot sustain its democracy on an abstract pact of never repeating the crimes of the past as long as the majority of the so-called "previously" disadvantaged are in fact still disadvantaged and take to violent measures to survive, since ideas like the burden of history, and the political ideals of democracy must have very little significance when viewed from below the poverty-line. True freedom, therefore, lies within the political as well as cultural and economic empowerment of the oppressed, in a thrust towards an open, egalitarian society. Only that will end the material, cultural and spiritual wretchedness of the South African majority.

To sum up, the representation of history in *Ways of Dying* passes a Jamesonian "rigorous judgement" on the present by the future and it does so in two ways. On the one hand, it offers an invitation to a conscientious use of the past that may redeem post-apartheid South Africa, as has been proposed by Ndebele. On the other hand, it offers a warning that any disregard of the past may result in a continued form of social, cultural and economic oppression.

# Conclusion

Although this book is far from being exhaustive in relation to its subject, the three novels that have been analysed do illustrate the scope and the complexity of historical fiction in post-apartheid South Africa. Whereas the previous anti-apartheid writing was predominantly focussed on depicting the realities of oppression, the contemporary authors of creative histories have used the liberation of literature to expand the range of themes boundlessly, from Serote's detailed portrait and psychological perusal of the resistance movement and Nicol's intellectual pursuit of other, literary rather than historiographic, apertures to the truth of the past to Mda's extension of the reach of historical themes into the corners of the social margin.

At the same time, the range of forms in which to represent these themes has been widened to span the literary spectrum from the realistic to postmodernism and magical realism. The choice of any of these forms, it has been shown, is intricately connected with the author's intention of addressing the given historical theme. Serote finds the realist convention suitable for conveying the kind of felt history required to establish a tangible idea of what life was like in the resistance. The technical similarity in Serote's realist style to conventional historical writing should be seen, moreover, in the context of the tradition between female and non-white writers to circumscribe their exclusion from authenticated history production by recording their own history in the creative genres. Nicol's postmodernist assaults on the discourse of history can, in turn, be regarded as a direct result of the close alliance between realist fiction and history writing in which the former has tended to be subordinated by the latter. The revolt against the master-narrative of history, then, constitutes an attempt to escape supplementarity in an assertion of the independence of literary discourse. Added to that, Nicol clearly feels an incapacity in traditional historical discourse of effectuating a lasting memory of pain and guilt. In fact, history as a mode of representing the past is founded on a logic that immanently advances the kind of departure from the past that allows for the repetition of past wrongs. The subversive potential in postmodernism may be employed to dismantle existing meaning-making structures and in that capacity it becomes an enabling factor in both arriving at a "truer truth" and offering an alternatively durable approach to remembering. Mda's resort to magical realism offers a stimulating departure from what may be seen as the fatigued European forms of realism and postmodernism while simultaneously encompassing both. The fusion of realism with magic induces the story with both the lived experience of Serote and the literary breakout from the discourse of history in Nicol. The result is a formidable attention-drawing effect that invites new ways of comprehending the country's history. For the same reason, the disruption of western rationality invites a change of consciousness that pushes the boundaries of what we conceive as possible. Finally, Mda's magical realism can be seen in connection with his purport of reviving an African aesthetic; literarily against the mentioned European forms and culturally against the shattering of African cosmologies by the course of history.

Thirdly, historical fiction in South Africa emerges as notably eclectic in that its historical conceptualisation embraces a holistic understanding of history as comprising the present and the future in addition to the past. Hence it has been shown how the historical novel has burst its traditional definitional confines of dealing with a period of the past, as in Serote, to include history as the present and the future, as in Nicol and Mda respectively.

However, the most remarkable feature of these novel histories is their capacity of using historical material to challenge post-apartheid South Africa by critically contributing to the discussion of how to shape the new democracy and its future. History is vitalised, in this way, from antiquarianism to a relevance of projection that shoulders the present.

The theoretical framework that has been applied to expound this critical dynamic in the three novels is Michael Green's concept of resistant form, the kernel of which is a use of history that resists the powers that be at any time. Rather than being exploited as a legitimisation of present power structures, as is the historiography of story, history, be it perceived as the past, present or future, is to be positioned as a point of difference that passes a perpetual and "rigorous" judgement on the present.

A brief probe into the popular mood of South Africa will elucidate the immediate necessity of deploying a use of history as resistant form. In her review of J. M. Coetzee's *Disgrace*, entitled "Our past still disgraces us", Anne McElvoy states that:

> The happy ending provided by the onset of democracy and the passing of apartheid is so comfortable, the delight in the triumph of the winds of change so great, that it has seemed impolite or ungrateful to raise the gravity of the future threats to the country's democracy and prosperity. If you think this sounds sour or harsh, look to the carefully sanitised popular imagery of post-apartheid South Africa, which relies on an idealised evocation of harmony in the townships. The most telling is the Heinz soup advert with the inevitable black church choirs creating the required heart-warming, home-coming effect. The fact that this could rely on us all having such a spontaneous mushy reaction to the music and imagery of a society few us know from our own experience is testament to South Africa's ability to embody the soothing myth of Good Times succeeding Bad (McElvoy, 1999: 29).

To allow one last analytical entry, Green says of the way our historical consciousness works that:

> We need to posit a point of conclusion…in order for what has come before to make sense; it takes shape only in relation to an end point which then allows for the organisation of what preceded it (248).

Against this backdrop, the dynamics at work in the contemporary sentiments that McElvoy refers to, the dynamics behind their very ability to lift the burden of history from the present, is precisely that the understood point of conclusion that is craved for by our historical consciousness is complacently set at the democratic elections in 1994. The same can be said about political strategies that legitimate present agendas by alleging that the past has been replaced by a rectified present. Such euphemising vocabulary come to mind as the *New* South Africa, the *New* National Party, the *previously* disadvantaged, the *previously* advantaged. By setting up 1994 as a point of conclusion our perception of historical time is organised as being severed between a past of hardship and pain and its deliverance at the moment the corrupt system is terminated. Or, as McElvoy puts it, the soothing myth is activated of "Good Times succeeding Bad".

The point is then that all the resistant forms that have been analysed in this study parry any indiscriminate celebration of the new dawn. Rather, they offer no redemption in the present, either by refraining from setting up a point of conclusion, as in Serote, or, as in Nicol and Mda, by postponing it to an indefinite future, reminding their fellow South Africans of "what they are not", "what they are no longer" and "what they are not yet". Instead of endorsing "all that is" – the politics or ideological currents of post-apartheid South Africa – they use their historical point of departure as an image of difference, an image, one might say, of an ideal or utopian other "in the midst of all", that judges the present conscientiously, politically and ideologically. To paraphrase McElvoy, they address the "gravity of the future threats to the country's democracy and prosperity", "ungratefully", "sourly" and "harshfully".

Summing up, Serote's affirmation of the resistance movement, of which the revisionary affinity carries the potential of endorsing the politics of the present government, resists such usage by centralizing the ordinary people who fought rather than the ANC itself. Instead of a victorious hindsight, Serote's narrative time stops short of the absolution of the struggle and he stimulates his characters with a scepticism towards even a liberated future. This appears presently as a watchdog installation, observing the manipulation of the political ideals for which the people sacrificed. Likewise Serote's, like Mda's, rendition of violations committed by the anti-apartheid movement itself resists any erection of a new censored national script. Nicol resists the contemporary forces of forgetting whether they be promoted by evasions of guilt by perpetrators, by cleaning the slate of the past with forgiveness, or by the closure that is forced upon the foregoing in the discourse of history. Contrarily he proposes a "truly tough aesthetic", like that of Derek Walcott, which neither explains nor forgives history in a perpetual judgement of the contemporaneity. In utopian terms, only by refusing to forgive the perpetrations of the past or settle the past by explaining the causalities that led to perpetration, will a new humanity be fostered that barricades the repetition of history. Finally, Zakes Mda resists the legacy of the past that may confer on the country an undesired course of development. He adds to Serote's political and Nicol's moral disputation a resistance of socio-cultural and economic dimensions. Utopian and dystopian visions of the future challenge the present by questioning whether Serote's political self-determination is truly autonomic unless it is rooted in cultural self-determination. And he adds to Nicol's notions of contrition the need for material redistribution, extending the responsibility for ending the need of economic empowerment to the present rulers and the emerging black middle class. The unreachable ideal that must nonetheless be striven for is a society of cultural, social, political and economic symmetry.

As truly resistant forms, none of the three novels assumes absolutist ends. All challenges are to evolve through continued explorations of what the pasts of South Africa have in stall for its futures. As such they accomplish what Ndebele sees as the finest function of literature:

> The power of creative writing is relevant for only there is language freed from its association with a purely manipulative function. The truth of literature is to be found in its power to allow readers to formulate insights independently

of outside authority to allow them to recreate themselves by enabling them to freely write their own texts (1994: 139)

Unlike conventional history that tells us in what direction to think about events, novel histories, when qualifying as resistant forms, invite readers to enact upon history autonomously and evaluate the present critically and self-critically (Hayden White paraphrased in Brink, 1996: 18-9). This may effect the kind of transformation of reader consciousness that contributes "to bringing about a highly conscious, sensitive new person in a new society" (Ndebele: 1994: 73).

That notion brings us back to the opening quotation of this book in which Ndebele urges us to address the past in this most crucial of times, as the past is "deeply embedded in the present" and to neglect it is to "postpone the future". Although apartheid is over constitutionally and in terms of a democratically elected government, the basic proposition in post-apartheid historical fiction is that the past will "continue to disgrace the future" of South Africa unless the development of South African society is strictly informed by the challenge and the judgement that is passed upon it by its composite histories.

# Notes

1. Malkki's study of the formation of Hutu mythico-histories is based on observations she made in Hutu refugee camps in Tanzania. She further explains that mythico-histories are not *mythical* in the sense of being made up:

> No doubt – as is the case with all myth, and all history – some narrative claims could be shown to be factually correct, and others not: But what made the refugees' narrative mythical, in the anthropological sense, was not its truth or falsity, but the fact that it was concerned with *order* in a fundamental, cosmological sense. That is the key. It was concerned with the ordering and reordering of social and political categories with the defining of self in distinction to other, with good and evil. It was most centrally a *moral order* of the world. It seized historical events, processes, and relationships, and reinterpreted them with a deeply moral scheme of good and evil (Malkki, 1995: 55-6).

2. Just how efficient the apartheid administration was, in consolidating its deliberate historical falsification beyond the borders of South Africa, occurred to me recently. An editor at a highly respected Danish publishing house asked me during the process of writing a book on South Africa for Danish school children to consider "the fact that the Boers arrived in South Africa before the Bantu."

3. Ranajit Guha counters the perception of historiography as "a realm of perfect neutrality" (Guha, 1983: 9). The appearance of historiography as a record of the "factual" vacated from comment and opinion is a deceptive pretence that has been carefully incorporated into its narrative style. As applies to all texts, the deconstruction of any historical text reveals a dependency on metonymy and metaphor which are both signifying strategies loaded with intention. Consequently, to paraphrase Guha, "facts" can never "speak for themselves" and Comment is bound to be worming its way through the armour plate of factuality (Guha, 1983: 13, 21).

4. In this respect, it should be noted in passing that although Michael Green will provide the overall theoretical framework, particularly two other critics, Njabulo Ndebele and J. M. Coetzee, will resurface now and again to debate the role of literature in general and the role of literature in relation to historical writing in particular. Especially Ndebele's call for a literature that involves as well as informs the reader will run through the book as will Coetzee's notion of a literature that may formally resist the discourse of history itself. Finally it will appear how Ndebele's urge for a conscientious use of history that may salvage tomorrow's South Africa (as it is expressed in the opening quote) seems to resound some of the thematics in Green's model of resistant form.

5. Legassick and Minkley even go as far as to say that to a great extent the objective of the Truth and Reconciliation Commission (TRC) to give voice to the silences of the past has already been reached by the social historians. The codes of the TRC of "hidden history", "marginal", "real", "objective", "new" are but echoes of the codes of social history, which, ironically, has been completely ignored by the TRC (123).

Furthermore, it is argued, the potential of the TRC, which would truly exceed the capacity of social history, to radically break down the divisions between elite and subaltern accounts through massive testimonies of personal memory, has been undermined by the commission's shift away from the emphasis on ordinary people to an increasing preoccupation with legal challenges and conspiracies at the top of the hierarchy coinciding with the evasions of especially P. W. Botha and Winnie Mandela (121-3).

6. The flaw in this study of not including a female writer among the main works is admitted appropriately. The only justification is that the works were selected not from a criteria of being representative of race, ethnicity or gender, but from requirements to the novels' form and content that, put together, would present the strands of realism, postmodernism and magical realism in conjunction with an elucidation of history as the past, present and the future.

7. The method of killing people by "necklacing" derives its name from the tyre that was filled with petrol, "perfume", and hung around the neck of the sentenced before set alight. Sindiwe Magona offers a thought-provoking comparison of the word with the act:

> The necklace. That is what we chose to call our guillotine. Necklace. What an innocent-sounding noun... Just as we kept on calling, insisted on calling, the people who did the necklacing 'children' 'students' 'comrades', we called a barbaric act the necklace, protecting our ears from a reality too gruesome to hear: clothing satanic deeds with innocent apparel.... Necklaced. Is it more palatable?" (77).

8. Sindiwe Magona's claim is indeed a valid one and can be substantiated by such rhetoric as has been recorded of Winnie Mandela: "Together, hand in hand, with our boxes of matches and our necklaces we shall liberate our country" (Meintjes, 1999: 222).

9. The whole process from repetition to parodic imitation was recognized in an interview with Mike Nicol while he was still writing *The Ibis Tapestry*:

> You are writing against existing books [official history and literary tradition]. And so, somehow, I feel there has to be a reference to that, and it does in the end result in parody, because I think what happened in postmodernism is that we lost our innocence" (Sevry, 1997: 101).

10. It is not the argument here that the dilemma between, on the one hand, representing the world in realist fashion and, on the other, revolting against the referential illusion with which historical discourse authorizes itself can be solved only through a third form like magical realism. Realism and epistemological scepticism are not at all mutually exclusive, which is demonstrated, for instance, by J. M. Coetzee himself in a few of his novels. *Age of Iron*, for example, depicts the sordid reality of state oppression in very concrete fashion while the politics of representing reality are debated in the main character's internal monologue. The other way round, a postmodernist re-invention of apartheid history like Chris van Wyk's *The Year of the Tapeworm* succeeds very well in channelling an unequivocal and tangible sense of the horrific in its depiction of the violence of South African history.

11. It should be noted that the vindication of African culture and aesthetics that is so

explicitly suggested in *Ways of Dying* seems only possible now that the retribalisation policies of the National Party are gone. During apartheid, it was considered an almost pro-government statement to claim one's ethnic heritage. Hence the outspoken self-negations of the *Drum* magazine at the height of resistance:

> Tribal music! Tribal history! Chiefs! We don't care about chiefs! Give us...anything American. You can cut out this junk about kraals and folk-tales and Basutos in blankets – forget it! You're just trying to keep us backward, that's what!

The reconsideration of this mentality in *Ways of Dying* is not an isolated case. Can Themba says: "Those of us who have been detribalised and caught in the characterless world of belonging nowhere have a bitter sense of loss (quoted in Gready, 1990: 147).

In post-apartheid South Africa even white authors have used the change to re-imagine Afrikaner or English identity by forging a cultural connection with indigenous tradition in a thrust to finally take root on the continent as Africans. The story of Krotoä, for instance, a Khoi-San woman who married and had children with the Danish surgeon Pieter van Meerhoff in the 17$^{th}$ century, resurfaces again in Afrikaner memory after its apartheid repression, as a myth of the unifying foremother, *onse ma*, who has fostered a fundamentally hybrid race (see Coetzee, 1998: 112-15). And in terms of literary form, works like Brink's *Imaginings of Sand* and Etienne van Heerden's *Ancestral Voices* are joining Zakes Mda by revalidating African traditions of story-telling and magic and mixing those with oral traditions among Afrikaners and the English settlers.

12. In the same way an uneasiness deriving from repression of the truth may be detected in the case of Noria's second pregnancy. The narrators never question her claim to divine conception despite the gossip of Noria seeing other men and gossip being one of the primary sources of the narrators' omniscience (140 and 8). Of course the possibility of a divine pregnancy serves the principle of presenting South African ontology as magic by taking magic for granted, or, as Faris puts it, to make it "grow organically out of reality" (106). However, the context of Noria's pregnancy invites an unnerving ambiguity. Just as much as the incident may be genuinely magic, the magic may also prove to be Noria's mind playing a self-deceiving trick. Considering the innumerous rapes that take place constantly in Noria's environment and considering the ambivalence of her many "dreams" of strangers that arrive to make love to her before she falls pregnant, the magical conception may turn out to be the poignant sign of a mental defence mechanism that is protecting Noria from the painful memory of being raped.

Antjie Krog refers to an almost conspiratorial silence about the issue of rape during the hearings of the Truth Commission:

> There seems to be a bizarre collusion between the rapist and the raped. Although rumours abound about rape, all these mutterings are trapped behind closed doors. Apparently high-profile women, among them cabinet ministers, parliamentarians and businesswomen, were raped and sexually abused under the previous dispensation – and not only by the regime, but by their own comrades in the townships and liberation camps. But no one will utter an audible word about it (277).

Although Noria of course belongs to a different level than the career-minded ministers and businesswomen, many reasons for keeping silent may be the same. A clinical psychologist, Nomfundo Walaza, adds "[w]ho have been raped know that if they talk about it in public they will lose something again – privacy, maybe respect" (277). The fact is that the silence of the public, which, in this interpretation, is represented in *Ways of Dying* in the absence of any response from the narrators to Noria's pregnancy, endorsing or rejecting the magic, preserves the issue of rape as a taboo or a violation that women have to endure privately. Even Serote's novel, which is so concerned with a female perspective of the past, is conspicuously silent about rape. Although the crime itself and the almost ritual repression of it in public, are, of course, far from problems that are confined to African societies, the culturally specific addressal in *Ways of Dying* concerns a skepticism towards the communal voice and its silences, and a skepticism towards self-righteous alignments by the same voices behind a pretense of Africanism as a moral high ground (see for instance Malungana, 1999 for an example of how uncritical Africanism can be exploited to championing the silencing of women).

13. The ideal way of instituting social modernization and development was touched upon by Bessie Head who stressed the necessity of indigenous incorporation – especially when the impulse of change was as foreign as the European. She made the following observation in Botswana:

> If one wishes to reach back into ancient Africa, the quality of its life has been preserved almost intact in Botswana.... Anything that falls into its depth is absorbed. No new idea stands sharply aloof from the social body, declaiming its superiority. It is absorbed and transformed until it emerges somewhere along the line as 'our traditional custom'. Everything is touched by 'our traditional custom' – British Imperialism, English, Independence, new educational methods, progress, and foreigners. It all belongs (Head, 1990: 15).

14. At this junction it would be appealing to amalgamate Coetzee and Ndebele's theories by stating that Ndebele's literature of involvement corresponds to Coetzee's rival mode. A consequence of such an argument would be that Ndebele's literature of informing equates the information that is passed on to the reader through the discourse of history. The parallels between Ndebele and Coetzee in this respect are pronounced but not convincing. First of all historical discourse may be as involving as informing in that there are consciousness-raising potential in the historian's choice of perspective for any given historical period. Secondly, consciousness-raising elements in literature do not necessarily move beyond the certain density of observation that Coetzee identifies in much historical fiction. It may be argued, for instance, that the probes into the psychology in Serote's characters and Lindi's attempts to redress the tormented minds around her add to the historical material a certain and engaging depth without taking up arms against the discourse of history itself.

15. It can be asserted against this argument that redistributive concessions have been imposed on the privileged after all, in the form of increased tax-rates (which prior to the year 2000 reform, in regard to income tax, amount to 45 % for the highest salaried groups (see South African Revenue Service: www.sars.gov.za/Default.htm). However, the new budget as presented by Minister of Finance, Trevor Manuel in February 2000 compromises these measures to a certain extent with new tax breaks for the employed. Jay Reddy's comment could furthermore be defended when arguing that taxing customarily loads the burden of redistribution unevenly on the middle-class and lower middle-class when considering the advantages of tax deductions that are always enjoyed

by the wealthy. As it was phrased in the editorial of the Mail & Guardian on the 25th of February 2000, in reference to Trevor Manual's promise of an asset sales tax directed against the rich (a cushion against the left-wingers' response to the tax reductions): "...the rich can afford to pay cunning accountants to help them avoid the worst strictures of the capital gains tax" (The Mail & Guardian, 2000; see also Barrell, 2000). In that light the greatest beneficiaries of the apartheid system are still able to circumvent their social responsibilities.

# Bibliography

Appiah, Kwame Anthony: "The Postcolonial and the Postmodern" in Bill Ashcroft, Gareth Griffiths and Helen Tiffin (eds.): *The Post-Colonial Studies Reader*. London: Routledge, 1995 (pp. 119-124).

Attridge, Derek and Rosemary Jolly: Introduction of *Writing South Africa. Literature, apartheid, and democracy 1970-95*. UK: Cambridge University Press, 1998 (pp. 1-13).

Attwell, David: "The Problem of History in the Fiction of J. M. Coetzee" in Martin Trump (ed.): *Rendering Things Visible. Essays on South African Literary Culture*. Johannesburg: Ravan Press, 1990 (pp. 95-133).

Barrell, Howard: "Budget Backs Business for Growth" in *Daily Mail & Guardian*, February 25, 2000 (www.mg.co.za/mg/news/2000feb2/ 25feb-budget2.html).

Braude, Claudia: "Elusive Truths" in *Mail & Guardian*, Friday (supplement) 12-18 June, 1998, p. 9.

Brink, André: "The past must not be laid to rest" in *The Weekly Mail* (Review of Books), 29 November – 5 December, 1991 (pp. 1 and 3).

Brink, André: "To re-imagine our history" in *The Weekly Mail & Guardian*, Review of Books, September 24-30, 1993 (pp. 1-2).

Brink, André: *Imaginings of Sand*. London: Minerva, 1997.

Brink, André: "Reinventing a Continent: Revisiting History in the Literature of the New South Africa: (A Personal Testimony)" in *World Literature Today. A Literary Quarterly of the University of Oklahoma*, Vol. 70, No. 1, 1996 (pp. 17-23).

Brink, André: "Interrogating Silence: New Possibilities Faced by South African Literature" in *Writing South Africa. Literature, apartheid, and democracy 1970-95*. UK: Cambridge University Press, 1998, (pp. 43-54).

Brydon, Diana: "The White Inuit Speaks. Contamination as Literary Strategy" in Bill Ashcroft, Gareth Griffiths and Helen Tiffin (eds.): *The Post-Colonial Studies Reader*. London: Routledge, 1995 (pp.136-142).

Chapman, Michael: *Southern African Literatures*. London and New York: Longman Limited Group, 1996.

Cobbet, William and Cohen, Robin (eds): *Popular Struggles in South Africa*. London: James Currey, 1988.

Coetzee, Carli: "Krotoä remembered: a mother of unity, a mother of sorrows?" in Sarrah Nuttal and Carli Coetzee (eds.): *Negotiating the past: The making of memory in South Africa*. Oxford and Cape Town: Oxford University Press, 1998, (pp. 112-19).

Coetzee, J. M.: *Age of Iron*. London: Secker & Warburg, 1990.

Coetzee, J. M.: *Disgrace*. South Africa: Random House (Pty), 2000 (First published in Great Britain by Martin Secker & Warburg, 1999).

Cohen, David William: *The Combing of History*. Chicago and London: The University of Chicago Press, 1994.
Cornevin, Marianne: *Apartheid: Power and Historical Falsification*. Paris: UNESCO, 1980.
Dangor, Achmat: "Just Before We Shall Sing" in *The Sunday Independent*, 4 February, 1996, (p. 22).
Dangor, Achmat: *Kafka's Curse*. Cape Town: Kwela Books, 1997.
Deegan, Heather: *South Africa Reborn*. London: UCL Press, 1999.
De Kok, Ingrid: "Standing in the Doorway: A Preface" in *World Literature Today. A Literary Quarterly of the University of Oklahoma*, Vol. 70, No. 1, Winter 1996, (pp. 5-8).
Driver, Dorothy: "Annual Bibliography 1992 and 1993" in *Journal of Commonwealth Literature*, Vol. XXIX, No. 3, 1994 (pp. 125-238).
Faris, Wendy B.: "Scheherazade's Children: Magical Realism and Postmodern Fiction" in Lois Parkinson Zamora and Wendy B. Faris (eds.): *Magical Realism. Theory, History, Community*. Durham and London: Duke University Press, 1995 (pp. 163-89).
Foreman, Gabrielle P.: "Past-On Stories: History and the Magically Real, Morrison and Allende on Call" in Lois Parkinson Zamora and Wendy B. Faris (eds.): *Magical Realism. Theory, History, Community*. Durham and London: Duke University Press, 1995 (pp. 285-303).
Goosen, Jeanne: *Not All of Us*. (Translated by André Brink) Cape Town: Queillerie Publishers Limited, 1992 (Afrikaans edition *Ons is nie almal so nie* by HAUM Literary Publishers, 1990.
Govender, Ronnie: *At the Edge and Other Cato Manor Sories*. Prestoria: MANX, 1996.
Gready, Paul: "The Sophiatown Writers of the Fifties: the Unreal Reality of Their World" in *Journal of Souther African Studies*, Vol. 16, No. 1, March, 1990 (pp. 139-65).
Green, Michael: *Novel Histories. Past, Present, and Future in South African Fiction*. Johannesburg: Witwatersrand University Press, 1997.
Head, Bessie: "Social and Political Pressures that Shape Literature in Southern Africa" in Cecil Abrahams (ed.): *The Tragic Life. Bessie Head and Literature in Southern Africa*. New Jersey: Africa World Press, Inc, 1990 (pp. 11-17).
Holiday, Anthony: "Forgiving and forgetting: the Truth and Reconciliation Commission" in *Negotiating the past: The making of memory in South Africa*. Oxford and Cape Town: Oxford University Press, 1998, (pp. 43-56).
Hutcheon, Linda: *A Poetics of Postmodernism: Story, Theory, Fiction*. London and New York: Routledge, 1988.
Hutcheon, Linda: *The Politics of Postmodernism*. London and New York: Routledge, 1989
Jones, Timothy Trengrove: "Novel probes into the workings of the truth commission" in *Sunday Times*, 13 September, 1998, (p. 23).

Krog, Antjie: *Country of My Skull*. UK and South Africa: Random House, 1999 (first published in South Africa by Random House, 1998).

Langa, Mandla: *The Naked Song*. Cape Town and Johannesburg: David Philip Publishers, 1996.

Lansink, Annette: "Forget revenge...what about compensation?" in *Sowetan*, 29 March, p. 9.

Legassick, Martin and Gary Minkley: "Current Trends in the Production of South African History" in *Alternation* 5, 1 (1998): 98-129.

Lundahl, Mats: "The Post-Apartheid Economy, and After?" in Lennart Petersson (ed.): *Post-Apartheid Southern Africa. Economic Challenges and Policies for the Future*. London: Routledge, 1998.

Magona, Sindiwe: *Mother to Mother*. Cape Town: David Philip Publishers, 1998.

Malungana, S. J.: "The Relevance of Xitsonga Oral Tradition" in *Alter*nation, Vol. 6, 1999, (37-54).

Manoim, Irwin: "Editorial" in *Weekly Mail & Guardian*, February 25, 2000: (www.mg.co.za/mg/news/2000feb2/25feb-budget8.html).

Maphai, Vincent T.: "Liberal Democracy and Ethnic Conflict in South Africa" in Harvey Glickman (ed.): *Ethnic Conflict and Democratization in Africa*. Georgia: The African Studies Association Press, 1998.

Marais, Hein: *South Africa: Limits to Change. The Political Economy of Transition*. South Africa: University of Cape Town Press, 1998.

Marlowe, Christopher: *Tambourlaine the Great*, 1587. Reprinted in Francis Cunningham (ed.): *The Works of Christopher Marlowe*. London: Chatto & Windus, 1902.

Marks, Shula and Stanley Trapido (eds.): *The Politics of Race, Class and Nationalism in the Twentieth Century South Africa*. London and New York: Longmans, 1987.

Marx, Anthony W.: *Lessons of the Struggle – South African Internal Opposition 1960 – 1990*. Cape Town: Oxford University Press, 1992.

McElvoy, Anne: "Our past still disgraces us" in *Saturday Argus*, 20-21 Nov., 1999, p. 29.

Meintjes, Sheila: "Winnie Madikizela-Mandela" in *They Shaped Our Century: The Most Influential South Africans of the Twentieth Century*. Cape Town, Pretoria, Johannesburg: Human & Rousseau, 1999.

Mervis, Margaret: "Fiction for Development: Zakes Mda's *Ways of Dying*" in *Current Writing*, Vol. 10, No. 1, 1998 (pp.39-55).

Mda, Zakes: *Ways of Dying*. Oxford and Cape Town: Oxford University Press, 1995.

Minkley, Gary and Ciraj Rassool: "Orality, memory, and social history in South Africa" in Sarrah Nuttal and Carli Coetzee (eds.): *Negotiating the past: The making of memory in South Africa*. Oxford and Cape Town: Oxford University Press, 1998, (pp. 89-99).

Moyo, Brian: "Exile and Home" (an interview with Mongane Wally Serote and Pitika Ntuli) in *Africa Events*, May 1990, pp. 53-4).

Naidoo, Venu: "Interview with Zakes Mda" in *Alter*nation, Vol. 4, No. 1, 1997 (pp. 247-61).

Ndebele, Njabulo: *South African Literature and Culture. Rediscovery of the Ordinary*. Manchester and New York: Manchester University Press, 1994.

Ngcobo, Dumisane: "Nihilism in Black South Africa: the New South Africa and the Destruction of the Black Domestic Periphery" in *Alternation*, Vol. 6, No. 1, 1999 (138-54).

Nicol, Mike: *The Ibis Tapestry*. New York: Alfred A. Knopf, Inc., 1998.

Ntantala, Phyllis: *A Life's Mosaic*: the Autobiography of Phyllis Ntantala. Cape Town: David Philip Publishers, 1992.

Oliphant, Andries: "Serote's style seeks its rationale in unadulterated song" in *Sunday Independent*, 18 July, 1999, p. 18.

Parry, Benita: "Speech and Silence in the Fictions of J. M. Coetzee" in *Writing South Africa. Literature, apartheid, and democracy 1970-95*. UK: Cambridge University Press, 1998, (pp. 149-165).

Raper, P. E.: *Dictionary of Southern African Place Names*. Rivonia: Lowry Publishers cc., 1987.

Russell, Diana: *Lives of Courage: Women for a New South Africa*. South Africa: David Philip Publishers, 1989.

Sachs, Albie: "Preparing Ourselves for Freedom" (1989 speech) in *Writing South Africa. Literature, apartheid, and democracy 1970-95*. UK: Cambridge University Press, 1998, (pp. 239-248).

Serote, Mongane Wally: *Gods of Our Time*. Randburg: Ravan Press, 1999.

Sevry, Jean: "An Interview with Mike Nicol" in *Commonwealth Essays and Studies*, Vol. 19, No. 2, 1997, (pp. 100-8).

Solberg, Rolf: "Interview with Mongane Wally Serote" in *Writing South Africa. Literature, apartheid, and democracy 1970-95*. UK: Cambridge University Press, 1998, (pp. 180-6).

Thompson, Leonard: *A History of South Africa*. USA: Yale University Press, 1990.

van Heerden, Etienne: *Ancestral Voices*. (Translated by Malcolm Hacksley) London: Penguin Books, 1981 (Afrikaans edition *Toorberg* by Tafelberg Publishers, Cape Town, 1986).

van Wyk, Chris: *The Year of the Tapeworm*. Johannesburg: Ravan Press, 1996.

van Wyk, Johan: "Catastrophe and Beauty: *Ways of Dying*, Zakes Mda's Novel of the Transition" in *Literator* 18 (3), Nov. 1997, pp. 79-90.

Walcott, Derek: "The Muse of History" in Bill Ashcroft, Gareth Griffiths and Helen Tiffin (eds.): *The Post-Colonial Studies Reader*. London: Routledge, 1995 (pp. 370-74).

Weekly Mail & Guardian: "Not the Last Word on the Truth" (no author indicated). October 30, 1998: (www.sn.apc.org/wmail/issues/ 981030/ NEWS23.html).

Zamora, Lois Parkinson and Faris, Wendy B.: "Introduction: Daiquiri Birds and Flaubertian Parrot(ie)s" in Lois Parkinson Zamora and Wendy B. Faris (eds.): *Magical Realism. Theory, History, Community*. Durham and London: Duke University Press, 1995 (pp. 1-11).